Richard Heber Newton

The Right and Wrong Uses of the Bible

Richard Heber Newton

The Right and Wrong Uses of the Bible

ISBN/EAN: 9783337171568

Printed in Europe, USA, Canada, Australia, Japan

Cover: Foto ©Lupo / pixelio.de

More available books at **www.hansebooks.com**

THE
RIGHT AND WRONG USES

OF

THE BIBLE.

BY

R. HEBER NEWTON.

RECTOR OF ALL SOULS' CHURCH (ANTHON MEMORIAL.) NEW YORK.

"In it *is contained* God's true Word."—*Homily on the Holy Scriptures.*

NEW YORK:
JOHN W. LOVELL COMPANY,
14 & 16 VESEY STREET.

WORKS BY THE SAME AUTHOR.

The Morals of Trade. 1 Vol. 12mo, cloth, gilt,   -   - $1.00

Studies of Jesus. 1 vol. 12mo, cloth, gilt,   -   -   -   -   1.00

Womanhood. 1 vol. 12mo, cloth, gilt,   -   -   -   -   1.25

The above will be sent by mail, postpaid, on receipt of price, by

JOHN W. LOVELL CO.

14 AND 16 VESEY ST., NEW YORK.

Copyright, 1883, by
JOHN W. LOVELL COMPANY.

Contents.

	PAGE
I. THE UNREAL BIBLE	7
II. THE REAL BIBLE	47
III. THE WRONG USES OF THE BIBLE	81
IV. THE WRONG USES OF THE BIBLE	105
V. THE RIGHT CRITICAL USE OF THE BIBLE	135
VI. THE RIGHT HISTORICAL USE OF THE BIBLE	169
VII. THE RIGHT ETHICAL AND SPIRITUAL USE OF THE BIBLE	221

" The Gospel doth not so much consist *in verbis* as *in virtute*."
JOHN SMITH.

"Liberty in prophesying, without prescribing authoritatively to other men's consciences, and becoming lords and masters of their faith—a necessity derived from the consideration of the difficulty of Scripture in questions controverted, and the uncertainty of any internal medium of interpretation."
JEREMY TAYLOR.

" To those who follow their reason in the interpretation of the Scriptures, God will either give his grace for assistance to find the truth, or His pardon if they miss it."
LORD FALKLAND.

[Rational Theology in England in the Seventeenth Century ; John Tulloch, D. D., II: 181, I: 398, I: 160.]

Preface.

It has been my custom for several years to give occasionally a series of sermons, having in view some systematic instruction of the people committed to my care. Such a series of sermons on the Bible had been for some time in my mind. With the recurrence of Bible-Sunday in our Church year, this thought crystallized in the outline of a course that should present the nature and uses of the Bible, both negatively and positively, in a manner that should be at once reverent and rational. In the course of this parochial ministration public attention was called to it in a way that has rendered a complete report of my words desirable.

The views set forth in these sermons were not hastily reached or lightly accepted. They represent a growth of years. Their essential thought was stated in a sermon that was preached and published eight years ago. My positions concerning certain books, etc., have been taken in deference to what seems to me the weight of judgment among the master critics. They are open to correction, as the young science of Biblical criticism gains new light. The general view of the Bible herein set forth rests upon the conclusions of no new criticism. In varying forms, it has been that of an historical school of thought in the English Church and in its American daughter. It is a view that has been recognized as a legitimate child of the mother Church; and that has been given the freedom of our own homestead, in the undogmatic language of the sixth of the Articles of Religion of the Protestant Episcopal Church. It is distinctly enunciated in the first sentence of the first sermon in the Book of Homilies, set forth officially for the instruction of the people in both of these Churches.

"Unto a Christian man there can be nothing more necessary or profitable than the knowledge of holy scripture, forasmuch as *in it is contained God's true word*, setting forth his glory, and also man's duty."

The whole controversy in Protestantism over the Bible may be summed into the question whether the Bible *is* God's word or *contains* God's word. On this question I stand with the Book of Homilies.

These sermons were meant for that large and rapidly growing body of men who can no longer hold the traditional view of the Bible, but who yet realize that within this view there is a real and profound truth; a truth which we all need, if haply we can get it out from its archaic form without destroying its life, and can clothe it anew in a shape that we can intelligently grasp and sincerely hold. To such alone would I speak in these pages, to help them hold the substance of their fathers' faith.

R. HEBER NEWTON.

ALL SOULS' CHURCH, *March* 1, 1883.

I.

The Unreal Bible.

"THE Bible, and the reading of the Bible as an instrument of instruction, may be said to have been begun on the sunrise of that day when Ezra unrolled the parchment scroll of the Law. It was a new thought that the Divine Will could be communicated by a dead literature as well as by a living voice. In the impassioned welcome with which this thought was received lay the germs of all the good and evil which were afterwards to be developed out of it : on the one side, the possibility of appeal in each successive age to the primitive, undying document that should rectify the fluctuations of false tradition and fleeting opinion ; on the other hand, the temptation to pay to the letter of the sacred book a worship as idolatrous and as profoundly opposed to its spirit as once had been the veneration paid to the sacred trees or the sacred stones of the consecrated groves or hills."

DEAN STANLEY : "History of the Jewish Church," iii. 158.

I.

The Unreal Bible.

"Forasmuch as many have taken in hand to draw up a narrative concerning those matters which have been fulfilled among us, even as they delivered them unto us, which from the beginning were eye-witnesses and ministers of the word; it seemed good to me also, having traced the course of all things accurately from the first, to write unto thee in order, most excellent Theophilus, that thou mightest know the certainty concerning the things which thou wast taught by word of mouth."—LUKE i. 1–4.

THIS day, in our Church year, calls us to think upon the influence of the Bible on the advance of man into the Kingdom of God.*
Since the growth of written language great books have been the well-springs of thought and feeling for mankind, from which successive generations have drawn the water of life. Since the introduction of the printing-press books have been, beyond all other agencies, the educators of men. And of all books of which we have any knowledge, those together constituting the Bible form incomparably the most potent factors in the moral and religious progress of the western world; and as all other progress is fed from moral and

---

* The Second Sunday in Advent.

religious forces, I may add, in the general advance of Christian civilization.

From these books the lisping lips of children have learned the tales of beautiful goodness which have nourished all noble aspirations. Over these charming stories of Hebrew heroism and holiness the imagination has caught sight of the infinite mysteries amid which we walk on earth. Their touch has quickened conscience into life. Through their voices the whispers of the Eternal Power have thrilled the soul of youth, and men have learned to worship, trust, and love the Father-God. These books have preserved for us the story of the Life which earth could least afford to lose, the image of the Man who, were his memory dropped from out our lives—our religion, morals, philanthropy, laws and institutions would lose their highest force. These books have taught statesmen the principles of government, and students of social science the cardinal laws of civilization. The fairest essays for a true social order which Europe and America have known have laid their foundations on these books. They have fed art with its highest visions, and have touched the lips of poesy that they have opened into song. They have voiced the worship of Christendom for centuries, and have cleared above progressive civilization the commanding ideals of Liberty, Justice, Brotherhood. Men and women during fifty generations have heard through these books the words proceeding from out the mouth of God, on which they have lived. Amid the darkness of earth, the light which has enabled our fathers to walk upright, strong for duty, panoplied against temptation, patient in suffering, resigned in affliction, meeting even death with no treacherous tremors, has shone from these pages. In their words young men and maidens have plighted troth each to the other, fathers and mothers have named their little ones, and by those children have been laid away in the earth in hope of eternal life. All that is sweetest, purest, finest, noblest in personal, domestic, social and civic life, has been fed perennially from these books. The Bible is woven into our very being. To tear it from our lives would be to unravel the fair tapestry of civilization—to run out its golden threads and crumble its beautiful pictures into chaos.

Yet we are threatened to-day with no less a loss than this. The Bible is certainly not read as of old. It is not merely the distraction of our busier lives, or the multiplicity of books upon our shelves, that turns men and women away from these classics of our fathers. Men and women no longer regard these books as did their fathers. They can no longer use them as their parents did; they see no other way to use them, and so they leave them unopened on their tables.

An intelligent lady said to me some time since:

"My children don't know anything about the Bible. I cannot read it to them, for I do not know what to say when they ask me questions. I no longer believe as I was taught about it: what, then, can I teach them?"

A confession which, if all parents were as frank, would have to be made in many other households. Where it is still used in home readings, it is, in hosts of houses, with the pain which mothers know when their children's honest questions cannot be as honestly answered.

Such a state of things is sad and dangerous. Unless some way be found to read these books without equivocation, they will gradually cease to be used in home instruction, and the coming generations will grow up without their holy influence. This state of things ought not to have been brought upon us. The reverent reading of the Bible alone would never have led us into such straits. It is the old story of all human reverence. That which we revere, we exaggerate. Glamor gathers around it. The symbol is identified with the spiritual reality. The image becomes an idol. The wonderful thing becomes a fetish. So we end in an irrational reverence of that which is worthy of a real and rational reverence. Then we have a superstition. Superstition always results in destroying the rightful belief of which it is the exaggeration and distortion.

This is the common story of superstition, from

the totemism of savage tribes and the image-worship of semi-civilized peoples on to the heathenism of the Mass. Men who felt the reality of a mystic communion with Christ, of which the Supper of the Lord was the symbol,—who felt the strengthening of their characters as their thoughts fed upon the words and life of Jesus, —naturally came to speak of the sacrament in terms of awe, which magnified the mystery, until at last they bowed down before the veritable body and blood of Christ, and trembled with fear as the tinkling of the silver bell announced that the priest was bringing God down into a wafer! They had really heard God speaking to them through the sacrament; and this never could have done them harm. But when they tried to express what they felt, they exaggerated and distorted the simple symbol of the Infinite Presence, identified it with the spiritual reality, and set up a Christian idol, a civilized fetish, which has done incalculable harm to men. The spiritual truth became an intellectual lie, and in every Catholic country superstition has eaten out faith, and reason refuses to reverence the sacrament.

The Bible has repeated this common story. The spiritual influence felt forth-flowing from it, the voice of God heard speaking through it, drew man's natural reverence to it. In trying to express the reasons for this reverence he has overstated and mis-stated the nature of these books.

The symbol has been identified with the reality. The Bible has become an idol, a fetish.

Bibliolatry, the worship of the Bible, is responsible for the lack of the reasonable reverence these sacred writings merit. This reasonable reverence can be recovered only by frankly putting away the unreasonable reverence. We must exorcise a superstition to save a faith. We must part with the unreal Bible if we would hold the real Bible. Iconoclasm is not pleasant to any but the callow youth. It may be none the less needful; and then the sober man must not shrink from shivering the most sacred shrine.

As runs the Hindu thought, the Destroyer is one of the forms of the Divine Power. God is continually destroying worlds and creeds alike; but in order to rebuild.

"Whose voice then shook the earth: but now he hath promised, saying, yet once more I shake not the earth only, but also heaven. And this word, Yet once more, signifieth the removing of those things that are shaken, as of things that have been made, that those things which cannot be shaken may remain."

According to its root-meaning, "learning" is a "shaking." Every new learning shakes society, now as in the days past. As the writer of the Epistle to the Hebrews saw, it is God who is shaking society in every such new learning, to the end that "those things which cannot be shaken may remain." Man need not fear to follow in the steps of God.

There is danger now in shaking men's faiths. There is danger, too, in leaving men's faith unshaken—unless the Divine process of progress is wrong. In the stress and storm of the tossing sea, Faith may go down in the waters. It may also die of dry rot by the old wharves. There is danger in rash utterance, but there is at least equal danger in timid silence. The time never comes when a reconstruction does not imperil some great interest. None the less the reconstruction must go on. Delay in pulling down may make building up of the old structure impossible.

As the story of past civilizations sadly shows, the gulf between the popular superstitions and the thoughts of scholars may widen until no bridge can span it, and religion perishes in it. It seems to me that the time has come when the pulpit must keep no longer silence. Its silence will not seal the lips of other teachers. Books and papers are everywhere forcing the issue upon our generation. Men's minds are torn asunder, their souls are in the strife. It behoves the Churches to remember that great word of Luther:

"It is never safe to do anything against the truth!"

When the venerable cathedral, in which our forefathers sought God and found Him, grows dangerously unsound; when its columns have crumbled and its arches have sprung, and its stout oaken timbers have dried into dust; the guardians of the sacred pile must plan its restoration as best they can. They must shore up its treacherous walls, take out its dead materials, carve new heads for the saints in the niches of the doors, build up the edifice anew, following faithfully as may be the old lines, and striving for the old spirit. When the scaffolding comes down, we may feel a shock of pain at the strange raw look of that which Time had stained with sacredness. But the minster has been saved for our children; and, when they shall gather within its historic walls, those walls will have grown venerable again with age, and they will not feel the loss which we have suffered, while as of old, they, too, shall hear the voice of God and find His Holy Presence.

I propose to consider with you, carefully but frankly, the real nature and the true uses of the Bible.

Let us examine to-day the traditional view of the Bible.

It is not easy to define the popular theory of the Bible. Like its kindred theory of Papal Infallibility, it is a true chameleon, changing constantly in different minds, always denying the absurdity of which it is made the synonym, ever qualifying itself safely, yet never ceasing to take on a vaguely miraculous character. Various theories are given in the books in which theological students are mis-educated, all of which unite in claiming that which they cannot agree in defining. The Westminster Confession of Faith may be taken as the dogmatic petrifaction of the notion which lies, more or less undeveloped and still living, in the other Protestant Confessions.

This Confession opens with a chapter "Of the Holy Scriptures," which affirms in this wise:

"The light of nature and the works of creation and Providence .... are not sufficient to give that knowledge of God and of His will, which is necessary to salvation. . . . . The authority of the Holy Scripture . . . . dependeth . . . . wholly upon God, the Author thereof; and therefore it is to be received, because it is the Word of God. . . . .

" . . . . and the entire perfection thereof are arguments whereby it doth abundantly evidence itself to be the Word of God, and establish our full persuasion and assurance of the infallible truth and divine authority thereof.

"The whole counsel of God concerning all things necessary for His own glory, man's salvation, faith, and life, is either expressly set down in Scripture, or by good and necessary consequence may be deduced from Scripture, unto which nothing at any time is to be added by new revelations of the Spirit.

"Being immediately inspired by God, and by His singular care and providence kept pure in all ages . . . . in all controversies of religion the Church is finally to appeal unto them."

The notion which the learned divines set forth so elaborately at Westminster, art has expressed in forms much better "understanded of the people." Mediæval illuminations picture the evangelists copying their gospels from heavenly books which angels hold open above them.

A book let down out of the skies, immaculate, infallible, oracular—this is the traditional view of the Bible.

Let me lay before you some of the many reasons why this theory of the Bible is not to be received by us.

I.

This theory has no sufficient sanction by the Church.

The Catholic or Œcumenical Creeds make no affirmation whatever concerning the Bible. This theory is found alone, in formal official statement, in the creeds of minor authority, the utterances of councils of particular churches; as, for example, in the Tridentine Decrees and the Protestant Confessions of Faith. There is no unanimity of statement among these several Confessions. Some of the Protestant Confessions of the Reformation era state this theory moderately. Some of them hold it implicitly, without exact definition. One at least is wholly silent upon the subject. The later creeds of Protestantism vary even more than the Reformation symbols. Such important Churches as the Church of England, our own Protestant Episcopal Church, and the Methodist Church have nothing whatever of this theory in their official utterances. These three Churches unite in this simple, practical, undogmatic statement (the sixth of the thirty-nine articles):

"Holy Scripture containeth all things necessary to salvation: so that whatsoever is not read therein, nor may be proved thereby, is not to be required of any man, that it should be believed as an article of the faith or be thought requisite or necessary to salvation."

II.

The Bible nowhere makes any such claim of infallibility for itself.

The prophets did indeed use the habitual formula, "Thus saith the Lord." So did the false prophets, as well as the true. It was the common formula of prophetism, indeed, of the Easterns generally when delivering themselves of messages that burned in their souls. The eastern mind assigns directly to God actions and influences which we Westerns assign to secondary causes. We are scientific, they are poetic. We reach truth by reasonings, they by intuitions. No one can follow the processes of the intuitions. To the mystic mind they are immediate illuminations from on high, inspirations of the Spirit of God. In the realm of law we trace the action of natural forces, and are apt to think there is nothing more. In the realm of the unknown we feel the supernatural, and are apt to think it all in all.

The great prophets themselves did not accept this language of other prophets unquestioningly. They denied the claim unhesitatingly when satisfied that the messages were not from on high. They distinguished between those who came in the name of the Lord; and so must we. They tried the spirits whether they were of God; bidding us therefore do the same.

Tried by the severest scrutiny of successive centuries, of different races, the great prophets prove to have spoken truly when they declared, of their ethical and spiritual messages, "Thus saith the Lord." If ever messages from on high have come to men, if ever the Spirit of God has spoken in the spirit of man, it was in the minds of these "men of the spirit." But they made no claim to infallibility, or if they did, took pains to disprove it. Every prophet who goes beyond ethical and religious instruction, and ventures into predictions, makes mistakes, and leaves his errors recorded for our warning. We must try even the inspired men, and when, overstepping their limitations, they err, we must say, Thus saith Isaiah, Thus saith Jeremiah.

No biblical writer shows any consciousness of such supernatural influences upon him in his work as insured its infallibility. Nearly all these authors begin and end their books without any reference to themselves or their work. The writer of the Gospel according to Luke thus prefaces his book:

"Forasmuch as many have taken in hand to draw up a narrative concerning those matters which have been fulfilled among us, even as they delivered them unto us which from the beginning were eye-witnesses and ministers of the word, it seemed good to me also, having traced the course of all things accurately from the first, to write unto thee in order, most excellent Theophilus, that thou mightest know the certainty concerning the things which thou wast taught by word of mouth."

This is the only personal preface to any of the Gospels, and it is thoroughly human. There is not even such an invocation as introduces Milton's great poem.

These writers at times, after the fashion of the older prophets, affirm that they speak with divine authority; but they also as expressly disclaim such authority in other places. St. Paul is sure, in one matter referred to him, of the mind of God, and writes:

"Unto the married I command, yet not I, but the Lord," etc.*

Immediately after he writes, as having no such assurance:

"To the rest speak I, not the Lord." †

Later on in the same letter he is so uncertain as to add to his judgment:

"And I think also that I have the spirit of God." ‡

Again, in the same connection, being conscious of no divine authorization, he gives his own opinion as such:

"Now, concerning virgins I have no commandment of the Lord, but I give my judgment." §

---

* 1 Cor. vii. 10. ‡ 1 Cor. vii. 40.
† 1 Cor. vii. 12. § 1 Cor. vii. 25.

Eighteen hundred years after he wrote, men insist that they know more about St. Paul's inspirations than he did himself. Against his modest, cautious discriminations, our doctors set up their theory of the Bible, clothe all his utterances with the divine authority, and honor him with an infallibility which he explicitly disclaims.

The New Testament writers use language which seems, to our theory-spectacled eyes, to ascribe an infallible inspiration to the Old Testament books. But the words have no such weight. The Epistle to the Hebrews opens with the words:

"God, who at sundry times and in divers manners spake in time past unto the fathers by the prophets," etc. *

The author of the Second Epistle of Peter writes:

"For the prophecy came not in old time by the will of man; but holy men of God spake as they were moved by the Holy Ghost." †

Such passages as these command the instant assent of all who reverence an ethical and spiritual inspiration in the prophets, and a real revelation through them, and they command no other belief.

In the first Epistle General of Peter we read:

"Concerning which salvation the prophets sought and searched diligently who prophesied of the grace that should come unto you ; searching what time or what manner of time the spirit of Christ which was in them did point unto, when it testified beforehand the sufferings of Christ and the glories that should follow them." ‡

---

* Hebrews i. 1.   † 2 Peter i. 21.   ‡ 1 Peter i. 10, 11.

Any idea of a progressive revelation implies that there was a light coming on into the world, which to them of olden time showed dimly a mystery into which they strove to look further. A vision of ideal goodness rose before them. It rested above the ideal Israel, chosen and called of God for a holy work. It shadowed that righteous servant of God with sorrow. The lot of the elect one was to be suffering. Thus the world was to be saved to God. This the great Prophet of the Exile saw. Christ's coming filled out this mystic vision, and it is fairly translated into the terms the Epistle uses.

The prophets were, in such lofty visionings, under an influence beyond their consciousness.

"The passive master lent his hand
To the vast soul that o'er him planned."

All other passages claimed in support of the notion of an infallible Bible fail on the witness-stand.

There is positively nothing in the New Testament which lends a reasonable countenance to such an amazing theory.

Even the stock argument, used when all other quotations failed, disappears in the honesty of the Revised New Testament. People who know no Greek see now that Paul did not write "All Scripture is given by inspiration of God"; but

" Every Scripture inspired of God is also profitable for teaching, for reproof, for correction, for instruction in righteousness."*

---

*2 Timothy iii. 16.

This is precisely the claim to be made for the Bible, as against the exaggerated notions cherished about it. It is good for—all forms of character-building. Its inspiration is ethical and spiritual. The test of the inspiration of any writing in it is its efficacy to inspire life with goodness.

III.

The Bible carries the refutation of this claim upon the face of its writings.

They thrust upon the attention of all who are not blind the traces of human imperfection, of a kind and an extent which precludes any notion of a clean copy of a perfect script let down from the skies.

The Old Testament historians contradict each other in facts and figures, tell the same story in different ways, locate the same incident at different periods, ascribe the same deeds to different men, quote statistics which are plainly exaggerated, mistake poetic legend for sober prose, report the marvellous tales of tradition as literal history, and give us statements which cannot be read as scientific facts without denying our latest and most authoritative knowledge. I shall not enumerate these "mistakes of Moses," and of others. That is an ungracious task for which I have no heart. It may be needful to remind the children of a larger growth, who persist in believing a saintly mother's beliefs to be final authority in their studies, that she is not infallible. But one does not care to catalogue her mistakes and taunt her with them.

That which carries no such reproach in it, but is, when rightly read, an honor to the Bible, may be pointed out, as the Biblical writers, indeed, do for us themselves.

The marks of a patient and noble literary workmanship are in every writing.

We can see this as our fathers could not see it, because the glasses through which to read literature critically have been ground within our century. Literary criticism is the study of literature by means of a microscopic knowledge of the language in which a book is written, of its growth from various roots, of its stages of development and the factors influencing them, of its condition in the period of this particular composition, of the writer's idiosyncrasies of thought and style in his ripening periods, of the general history and literature of his race, and of the special characteristics of his age and of his contemporary writers.

Every educated person knows something of the working of this criticism on other books. You have read your Shakespeare with intelligence, and have felt many misgivings as to the genuineness of a few plays, and of passages in many plays. The brutalities and beastlinesses of Titus Andronicus seemed impossible to the author of "The Tempest" and the "Midsummer Night's Dream." The historic plays seemed to you often "padded." But there was nothing more than guess-work in your conclusions, and, you suspected, in the more pretentious opinions of others. You take up, however, the lectures of Hudson or the charming study of Dowden, and you find that criticism is becoming, not merely an art, depending on certain instincts and tastes, but a science, building slowly a well-settled body of laws and rules, and shaping already a well defined consensus of judgment. The growth of the English language and literature, the characteristics of society, of language and of literature in the Elizabethan era, the idioms of Shakespeare's contemporaries, the manner of Shakespeare himself, in his different periods, have all been so minutely studied as to form a distinct specialty in knowledge. The Shakespearian scholar is a well differentiated species of the genus scholar, and speaks with a substantial authority upon what is now a real science. You can follow this teacher into Shakespeare's work-shop, watch the building of his plays, distinguish the hands which toiled over them and mark their journeyman's work, till quite sure where the Master's own inimitable touch caressed them into noble form, and in what period of his life he thus wrought. There is a new revelation of Shakespeare to our age.

This criticism turned upon the great books of the ancients. Niebuhr led the way in reconstructing the early history of the Romans. Dr. Arnold predicted that a Niebuhr of Jewish literature would arise. He came duly. His name was Ewald. Successors have followed in abundance. The principles and processes of literary criticism were applied to the Hebrew writings.

In the present immature stage of this science of Biblical Criticism there are, of course, plenty of speculations and guesses, of hasty generalizations and crude opinions. Time will correct these. Meanwhile there is already so much that may claim to be well established as to constitute a new knowledge of these old books.

The historical books are seen to be the work of many hands in many ages. They gather up the popular traditions of the race, carry down on their slow streams fragments from such far back ages that we have almost lost the clue to their story—glacial boulders that now lie strangely out of place in the rich fields of later eras; songs of rude periods, nature myths, legends of semi-fabulous heroes,-folk lore of the tribes, scraps from long-forgotten books, entries from ancient annals, pages torn from the histories of other peoples to fill out the story; the whole worked over many times by many hands in many generations.

Just as Thirlwall and Grote give us studies of Grecian history from the standpoint of Monarchism and Republicanism, so in the Kings and Chronicles we have studies of Hebrew history from a prophetic and priestly point of view.

The legislation of the Pentateuch, supposed formerly to have been drawn up by Moses, appears, as it now stands, to be a codification, made as late as the period of the Babylonian exile, under the influence of the hierarchical and ritual system, then crystallizing into the form familiar to us all. This codification, like its famous parallel in Roman history, the code of Justinian, collated the decisions and decrees already in existence from various periods, and reissued them as one body of laws.

It brings together the "Judgments" of early days upon questions of civil life—the decisions of tribal heads concerning the rights of person and property, the counterparts of the "Dooms" of English history; the moral rules of the local priests in a simple state of society; and the ritual and discipline of a late ecclesiastical age. The compilation is not very skilfully done, so that we pass from the minutiæ of a priest's *vade mecum* in a highly developed hierarchical period to the civil statutes of a rude patriarchal society, whose very crimes are archaic.

The prophecies break up into fragmentary collections, in which the words of many different and obscure prophets are grouped under the name of some great prophet, as was quite natural in an uncritical age; the whole mass being arranged with little chronological order.

The Psalter separates into several books of sacred song, dating from different periods. They repeat the same Psalm, and divide one Psalm into two and join two into one, on principles by no means apparent to us. Some of these Psalms are of a highly artificial and mechanical structure. There are acrostics, in which the couplets begin with the successive letters of the Hebrew alphabet; double acrostics, and other refinements of literary ingenuity; the sure signs of a flamboyant and decadent literature.

The other writings of the Old Testament and the books of the New Testament have yielded similar general results to the touchstone of criticism; concerning which it is needless to speak further.

Our critical glasses bring out, clear and strong, the fact of a human, literary craft in these books, the signs on every hand of the labor of brain and skill of pen through which the literature of a venerable nation, and of the infant church born of it, took slow shape into our Bible. Such a work needs must have in it the traces of human imperfection; and these limitations of thought and knowledge, these mistakes of fallible writers, are to be seen by every one, save those who will not see.

It is impossible after such a study to rest in the

illusion of an infallible book, of which, as a book, God can be said to be the "author."

IV.

The growth of this theory is plain to us, and discredits its authority.

The explanation that Max Müller makes of the growth of superstitious reverence for ancient traditions in Hindu history is suggestive on this point.

"In an age when there was nothing corresponding to what we call literature, every saying, every proverb, every story handed down from father to son received very soon a kind of hallowed character. They became sacred heir-looms, sacred because they came from an unknown source, from a distant age. There was a stage in the development of human thought when the distance that separated the living generation from their grandfathers or great-grandfathers was as yet the nearest approach to a conception of eternity, and when the name of grandfather and great-grandfather seemed the nearest expression of God. Hence what had been said by these half human, half divine ancestors, if it was preserved at all, was soon looked upon as a more than human utterance. Some of these ancient sayings were preserved because they were so true and so striking that they could not be forgotten. They contained eternal truths, expressed for the first time in human language. Of such oracles of truth it was said in India that they had been heard, Sruta, and from it arose the word Sruti, the recognized term for divine revelation in Sanskrit." *

How, in later times, the great writings of the Hebrews came to acquire the same exaggerated sacredness, we can also observe. We read in one of the historical books of the Jews that "Nehemiah founded a library and gathered together the writings concerning the Kings, and of the prophets, and the (songs) of David and epistles of Kings concerning temple gifts."† This formation of a National Library was really the germ out of which grew the Old Testament. It was a purely civic act by a layman, but it expressed the honor in which the national writings were coming to be held. It is coincident with this that we find a priestly movement to draw a sacred line around the more important writings of the nation.

Tradition has credited Ezra, the priestly coadjutor of Nehemiah, with the first formation of the Old Testament Canon. The two traditions express one and the same fact from the secular and ecclesiastical points of view. In the exile, the stricken nation came to value and honor its national heritage as never before. Its literary sense was quickened by close contact with the

---

* Sacred Books of the East, vol. i. p. xiii.
† 2 Maccabees, ii. 13.

civilization of Babylonia, whose great library constituted one of the chief treasures of the central city. It was natural that on their return to their native land the Jews should gather their race-writings and found a National Library.

The genius of Israel had always been religious. Its very literature was pre-eminently religious. That their venerable writings should be received as sacred was thus wholly natural. They were in reality sacred writings.

Moreover, a large part of these writings, and that part largely drawn from very ancient times, was composed of judicial decisions, legislative codes, etc., around which veneration properly gathered. This veneration was heightened by the popular traditions which assigned to Moses the bulk of their legislation, and traced it through him to Jehovah himself. During the exile a remarkable priestly development, which had been running on through two centuries, at least, culminated in a completely organized hierarchy and an elaborate cultus.

In the process of this final development in Babylonia the legislation and histories of the nation were worked over by priestly hands in the priestly spirit. The law of Moses was now for the first time completely set before the people, and on the restoration to Judea was made the law of the land. It became, therefore, in a new sense sacred.

The fresh, free inspirations of the prophets—inspirations most real and divine—died out in the exile, smothered partly by this priestly development.*

When no living prophet arose to make men hear the voice of God, men had to hearken for that voice in the words of the dead prophets. In the synagogues or meeting-houses which developed during the exile, when the holy temple was in ruins, and which, having been found useful, were continued in the restoration, the writings of the prophets were read each Sabbath. The true writings of the chief prophets had therefore to be indicated. Thus came the canon of the prophets.

The freedom with which the author of the Chronicles used the material of the older historians, which had been taken up into the sacred writings, shows that the sacredness attached to them had not isolated them into extra-human writings even a century and a half after Ezra.

The process of exaltation was at work, however, and continued thenceforth through the national history, increasing as the life of the nation ebbed. It was the period immediately following the destruction of Jerusalem by the Romans, which busied itself in closing the canon of Jewish Scriptures. Death bound up that Bible. No new chap-

---

* "The Jews and the priests have found it good that Simon shall be their leader and high priest forever until there shall arise a trustworthy prophet."—1 Macc. xiv. 41.

ters could be added, because there was no more life left to write them. In its dotage this noble nation became known, by its superstitious reverence for the law, as "the people of the book." Learned doctors gravely taught their pupils that "God himself studies the law for the first three hours of every day."

The superstitious exaltation of the sacred writings, coincident with the lapsing life of the nation, was partially responsible for it, as it discouraged the fresh inspirations of the soul, and suppressed all free spiritual thought.

The genesis of the similar theory concerning the Christian Scriptures repeats the story told above.

The formation of the Christian Church was a period of astonishing literary productivity, commensurate in extent and worth with the importance of Christianity. It was a creative epoch in history. The life and teachings of Jesus stirred the minds and thrilled the souls of men. The higher spheres brooded low upon our world. Spiritual influences of unparalleled magnitude were working in society. The "Spirit of God moved upon the face of the waters."

Writings of all sorts abounded. They carried such weight as their author's name or their intrinsic worth imparted to them. Even the most valuable were not so prized or guarded as to prevent some of them from being lost. Paul's own letters suffered from this neglect. Had a few copies of these inestimable letters been made by the churches to whom they were sent such a fate could not have befallen any of them. These writings were quoted freely by the early fathers, who rarely cared to give the exact language even of the great apostle.

As the churches multiplied and organized, the need of selection from the multitudinous literature of Christianity was felt. Genuine letters had to be distinguished from spurious letters. Accurate knowledge of the life and teachings of Christ had become a vital necessity. The growth of legend and fable, in the Apocryphal Gospels, threatened to swallow up the memory of the real Jesus. A sifting process went on in the churches, by which the unimportant and objectionable writings were gradually winnowed out and the wheat retained.

The Christian consciousness tried and tested every writing, accepting those which approved themselves inspired by inspiring.

In the course of time this thoroughly vital process, through which public opinion passed upon the Christian writings, was recorded officially in the legislative action of councils, and thus, after many incertitudes and vacillations, the selection of sacred writings was finished and the New Testament canon was closed. It was closed, as in the case of the canon of the Old Testament, by the gradual loss of free spiritual and literary productivity; closed, as the visions fade and the tides fall within the soul, and the period of criticism follows the period of creation.

These writings became rightly sacred as the mementoes of the Divine Man, and the counsels of the great apostles; a shrine in which men drew near to the supreme manifestation of God upon earth. But they became wrongly sacred also, as the lengthening lapse of time isolated these precious heirlooms of the Christian household into relics it was blasphemy to criticise; as the falling waters of the river of life stranded high above men's reach the thoughts and experiences of the inspired fisher-folk of Galilee. In the Dark Ages, when to read was a sign of distinction, and to write a schoolboy history like "Eginhard's Charlemagne" was a prodigy; when to lead clean lives, and to labor as hosts are doing now for their fellows, made a man a saint; the literary and spiritual power of the apostles was nothing less than preternatural.

In the Reformation the old story repeated itself.

In the days of fresh inspiration men surely did not fail to prize the blessed books whence had come their new life. But the sense of the divine life in their own spirits enabled them to judge of the inspiration of the Apostles at once reverently and rationally. They did not hesitate to criticise freely the sacred books. Erasmus wrote of the Revelation:

"I certainly can find no reason for believing that it was set forth by the Holy Spirit. . . . Moreover, even were it a blessed thing to believe what is contained in it, no man knows what that is. . . . But let every man think of it as his spirit prompts him." *

Luther wrote of the Epistle of James,

"In comparison with the best books of the New Testament, it is a downright strawy epistle." †

The ebbing tide again left the second generation critical and not creative. After the sages and prophets of Protestantism came the scribes and doctors, and they were concerned not so much with the manly religion of free learning which Erasmus cherished, or the ethical and spiritual religion which Luther roused, as with establishing Protestant*ism* and waging its doctrinal controversies. They wanted an authority for faith and morals to set over against the authority of Rome. The age knew of no other authority than external, extra-natural, official authority, the king by divine right in the realm of thought. In the place of the authority of the Church rose the authority of the Bible; an oracular, infallible, miraculous Book, instead of an oracular, infallible, miraculous Church. Men could only sustain the elaborate speculative system they had spun out of the New Testament letters, by insisting upon the authority of the

---

* Introduction to the New Testament. Samuel Davidson, I.: 279.

† Introduction to the New Testament. Samuel Davidson, I.: 334.

apostles in metaphysics as strongly as upon their authority in ethical and spiritual principles. When dogma became divine, the books whence it was drawn were deified.*

We simply enter into the heritage of the men who spent two and a half years in elaborating the Westminster Confession, the first chapter of which petrified this superstitious theory of the Bible. Profoundly as we reverence these truly sacred books, for the real revelation they record as coming in the spirits of holy men who spake as they were moved of the Holy Ghost, and supremely in the person of the Son of Man; and rightly as we recognize a Providential purpose in the preparation of these books for the guidance of human life; the history of these same thoughts and feelings in the past should warn us from renewing ancient exaggerations, injurious to the best influence of the Bible.

v.

This theory is incapable of a statement which is not self-stultifying.

To be an infallible authority upon all the matters upon which it treats, a book must not only be guaranteed in its thought. Thought changes more or less in finding an expression.

---

* The contrast between the fifteenth and sixteenth century Confessions of Faith reveals this process, and explains the prevalent Protestant theory.

No two statements of an idea or of a fact can be exactly alike. There are no real synonyms. Interchangeable words have each a special shade of meaning. The guarantee must cover the phraseology of the original language in which the book is written. The words must be dictated to amanuenses. The thorough-going verbal inspirationists are the only logical defenders of infallibility.

But the guarantee would need to be pushed still further in the case of a book written as was the Bible. The best stenographers make mistakes in filling out their abbreviations and in distinguishing the similar signs which stand for very dissimilar sounds. Early Hebrew was a language of abbreviations. No vowels were used. Consonants stood alone, and their conjunction, aided by memory, was expected to suggest the proper vowel accompaniments. Vowel points were added to the written language centuries after the last book of the Old Testament was written.* Their insertion demanded a guarantee, if infallibility was to be secured.

This guarantee must then have followed every copyist in the original tongues, every translation of the Hebrew and Greek into other tongues, every copyist in modern tongues through the ages before the printing-press, every printer, who, since Gutenberg, has issued a Bible—if we are to

---

* About 600 A.D.

be absolutely sure of having an oracular and an infallible Book.

The Westminster Confession, indeed, seems to follow its theory through most of these lengths, and a Protestant Council in Geneva in 1675, with a magnificent courage of conviction, actually affirms this supernatural direction of the translators of the Bible. But such notions are of the same nature with the preposterous traditions of the Jews, as to the translation of the Septuagint; according to which, seventy elders, separated from each other, produced seventy versions, which, on comparison, "agreed exactly"; whereby men knew that the Scriptures were "translated by the inspiration of God." With such tales we must leave the theory they seem necessary to authenticate in the lumber-loft of superstitions.

VI.

This theory of our Bible is, in our age, seen to be the same theory which all peoples have entertained of their bibles.

For the first time in the history of Europe, Christian people have the knowledge by which they can correct their ideas about the Bible, in what may be called a comparative science of Bibliolatry. We know that nearly every race has had its own Sacred Book. These Sacred Books are now within the easy reach of all.

Any one can examine for himself the Vedas, the Zend-Avesta and the other Bibles of humanity. Every one can readily form a just judgment of these Bibles. The light which lighteth every man that cometh into the world shines from many pages in all of these books. There are profound thoughts of God, noble ethical ideals, deep perceptions of sin, yearning desires for human good, gleams of life beyond the grave. There are prayers we could use here with a few verbal changes, and you would not recognize their pagan source. There are songs of praise which might be made our canticles. There are parables that the Master Himself might have spoken. But the light which shines from heaven through these books does not disguise their earthly character. Having no glamor of tradition over our eyes, we can see them to be histories, poems, philosophies, rituals, counsels of religion, hallowed by age into Sacred Books.

Yet we find precisely the same notions current in each race about its Bible that we have cherished concerning our own Bible. The Hindu talks of his Vedas as the Christian talks of his Testaments. Nay, we find our conceits quite outdone in the dogmas of these heathen. Mohammedan doctors of divinity divided into fiercely contesting parties over the question whether the Koran was created or uncreated; the latter theory, as most highly magnifying their Sacred Book, of course, becoming the orthodox doctrine. These learned orthodox divines assured men that the Koran was verily eternal and uncreated, and of the very essence of God; that the first transcript of it had been from everlasting by His throne; that a copy, in one volume, on paper, was, by the hands of the angel Gabriel, sent down to the lowest heaven in the month of Ramadân; from whence Gabriel revealed it to Mohammed in instalments, giving him the privilege, however, of beholding the heavenly volume, bound in silk and adorned with gold and precious stones, once a year.

We cannot mistake the fact that thoroughly human writings have been exaggerated into superhuman scriptures by the deference rightly called forth towards these venerable books, so influential in the histories of nations, so potent in the lives of men; and we can study the phases through which a wholesome reverence degenerated into a puerile superstition.

Bibliolatry is pushed to a *reductio ad absurdum* in these pagan worships of their Sacred Books. Men will see their folly in the reflected light of these kindred follies, and another superstition will disappear from Christendom.

On these grounds, as on others, the unreal Bible must be expected to pass away. The Church at large never properly authenticated it. The Bible nowhere calls for such a view of itself. Scripture reveals to a critical study manifest tokens of its human fallibility, its thoroughly literary character. We can trace the growth of this theory, and account for it naturally. As a theory it cannot be stated reasonably. It is a theory which is shown to be a superstition in the bibliolatries of other peoples.

Our bibliolatry is disappearing none too fast. It has always wrought evil as well as good on civilization. Like all other anachronisms, its original helpfulness to progress has now become a hindrance. The day when it was of service is past for educated people, whose minds are open, and the evils it has caused flow from it still.

It has bred a superstitious use of the Bible which has always made mischief, though a mischief never realized as sensibly as now. It has taught men to turn to these holy books and accept unquestioningly all therein recorded as authoritative on our thought and life. It has barred all research which even seemed to contradict its history or science, and has held Europe in mental swaddling-bands, preventing normal growth. It has taught Most Christian Kings to war with easy consciences, after the fashion of the Israelites in Canaan, and priests to sing solemn *Te Deums* over battle-fields where men lay weltering in one another's blood. It has given slave-owners the coveted proof that the peculiar system was a divine institution, and has founded the auction block for human cattle solidly upon the laws of God. It has supplied Joseph Smith with a warrant for polygamy in the social usages of the Arab sheiks three thousand years ago. It has opened a sacred refuge for every lie and wrong; no wildest form of which could fail to find some precedent within these Hebrew histories, which tell the story of a people's upward growth from savagery. It has furnished an arsenal stocked with proof texts, from which, through many generations, priests and doctors have armed themselves to war with one another; exhausting in ecclesiastical and theological strife the holy energies of Christian enthusiasm, which might else have changed the face of the earth. It has arrayed faith against reason, by the necessity it has imposed of reconciling every new discovery with the cosmogony of Genesis, or the metaphysics of Romans; putting asunder those whom God hath joined together, in the needless conflict of science and religion.

It has driven away from the real revelation held in these sacred writings increasing numbers, in the growing generations; deafening their ears by its irrational clamor to the voice of the Living God which whispers in these pages, through the holy men who spake as they were moved of the Holy Ghost. It has fathered the doubt which to-day sits, cheerless and chill, within the hearts and homes of thousands who once rejoiced in the warmth and light of God, but who now accept the alternative their teachers thrust upon them—"all or none"—and throw away the Blessed Book wherein God of old revealed Himself to them.

It has made the sacred ark of Israel so vulnerable that its defenders dare not challenge the great Goliath of the Philistines, who, year by year, comes forth to strut before the armies of the saints in ridicule of that they hold so dear; and thus it is to be held responsible for the loss of the young men who throw away their ancestral faith and go over to the apparently victorious side of Unbelief.

It has slid in a false bottom to men's faith; shoving in a supposititious revelation of miracle above the real revelation which is in nature and in man, and in the Christ as the ideal man; and thus holds back that reconstruction of belief which Providence is forcing on, as It is shaking all things, to settle faith upon the everlasting verities: whereon religion, planting its feet on the solid rock, may lift its head into the skies, and worship Him in whom we live, and move, and have our being, the God and Father of our Lord Jesus Christ, "Our Father who art in Heaven."

In the name of religion let it die!

Then there will be a resurrection, and the Bible will live again, clothed in a higher form for our most rational reverence. All that ever made the Bible a Sacred Book, lives on to-day and will live on while these books exist. Holy men of old spake as they were moved of the Holy Ghost. They were most truly inspired. The Biblical writers recorded a real revelation. These books hold for us the words of God. The Word of God speaks to us in the person of Jesus Christ.

These spiritual realities, no criticism can touch. And these spiritual realities make the Bible.

Book of our Fathers, venerable and sacred, speak still to our souls those words proceeding from out the mouth of God on which man liveth!

II.

The Real Bible.

> " Out from the heart of nature rolled
> The burdens of the Bible old;
> The litanies of nations came,
> Like the volcano's tongue of flame,
> Up from the burning core below,—
> The canticles of love and woe.
>
>   * * * * *
>
> The passive Master lent his hand
> To the vast soul that o'er him planned.
>
>   * * * * *
>
> Himself from God he could not free."
>
> *The Problem.*

"Holy men of God spake as they were moved by the Holy Ghost."—2 Peter, i. 21.

THE most original book in the world is the Bible. . . . The elevation of this book may be measured by observing how certainly all observation of thought clothes itself in the words and forms of speech of that book. . . . Whatever is majestically thought in a great moral element instantly approaches this old Sanscrit. . . . People imagine that the place which the Bible holds in the world it owes to miracles. It owes it simply to the fact that it came out of a profounder depth of thought than any other book.—EMERSON, *The Dial*, October, 1840.

II.

The Real Bible.

"MEN of the Scriptures" was the title assumed by the Karaites, a sect of devout Jews, who, about the middle of the eighth century of our era, threw aside tradition, and accepted as their sole authority the canonical writings of the Old Testament. Seeing the good that the Bible has wrought for man in the past, we may well emulate the reverence of these Karaites; while, seeing the unreality of the traditional notion of the Bible that they held, and the mischiefs it has bred, we may well disown their superstitiousness. Can we gain a view of the Bible which, without stultifying our intellectual nature, may satisfy our spiritual nature, and leave us free to call ourselves men of the Scriptures? The only road to such an end must be that which our age is opening so successfully through every field of study; as, dismissing preconceptions, it builds with care and candor, upon solid facts, the causeway to a certain knowledge.

Let us take up the Bible as we would any other collection of books, and see if, without assuming anything concerning it, we cannot find our way to a rational reverence for it, as real as that which our fathers had. The lines of our inquiry have been projected by a hand you own as high authority. The results of the survey are in the text. Real men wrote real books; holy men wrote holy books; and, when we come to account for their holy, human power, we can only say—The Divine Spirit stirred in them; "holy men of old spake as they were moved of the Holy Ghost."

The Bible is a collection of many writings, in many forms, by many hands, from many ages. Genuine letters these, whether they be *belles-lettres* or not; by every mark and sign most human writings, whether they be holy Scriptures or not; the product of honest toil of brain and hand. Whatever more they are, these are *bona fide* books, of men of like passions and infirmities with ourselves.

What is there in these books which has led Christendom to assign to them so high an honor?

I.

1. *These books have the venerableness which belongs to ancient writings.*

With what interest and care we handle a very old book, and turn its well-worn pages, thumb-marked and dog-eared by men of Oxford or of Florence in the Middle Ages! Unless we are the baldest materialists, we will not reserve for the parchment body of some old book the respect called forth by its soul. The latest re-embodiment of an ancient writer, fresh from the presses of Putnam or of Appleton, merits the honor belonging to the book given to the world so many centuries ago, and fed upon by successive generations. Thus I look at the Plato on my shelves. How venerable these writings! Over their great words, on which I rest my eyes, my fathers bent, as their fathers had done before them; generation after generation finding inspiration where still it flows fresh and full for me. Thus every reverently minded man ought to feel concerning the Bible. The latest of these books is probably seventeen hundred years old, and the earliest has been written twenty-seven hundred years; while in the more ancient of these writings lie bedded some of the oldest fragments of literature known to us. These books have been the constant companions of men and women through two or three score of generations. The crawling centuries have carried these books along with them—the solace and the strength of myriad millions of our kind. Forms now turning into dust, holy in our memories, read these familiar pages. Men whose names carry us back through English history knew and prized these writings; Cromwell, Shakespeare, Chaucer, and the Great Alfred. When Rome was the seat of empire, Constantine heard them in his churches. Aurelius informed himself about them.

In the lowly hamlet hidden away among the hills of Galilee, the boy Jesus listened to these tales of Hebrew heroism and holiness from His mother's lips. Judas, the hammerer, fired his valiant soul from them; and, while wandering in the hill country of Judæa, David chanted, to his harp's accompaniment, these legends of the childhood of his race. The Bible is hallowed by the reverent use of ages.

2. *These books form the literature of a noble race.*

The Old Testament is a Library of Jewish Letters. The germ of the collection was planted by Nehemiah, when "he, founding a library, gathered together the acts of the kings, and the prophets, and of David, and the epistles of the kings concerning the holy gifts.* This germ grew gradually into its present shape. The Apocrypha belongs to it, and is rightly bound up in our Bibles, for reading in our churches. These books of the Canonical and Apocryphal writings do not cover the whole literature of the Hebrew nation. Many writings have been lost inadvertently. Many have been dropped as unworthy of preservation. We have the garnered grain of Hebrew literature in our Bible—a winnowed national library. It includes histories, juridical codifications, dramas of love and destiny, patriotic songs and state anthems, the hymnal of a people's worship, philo-

---
* 2 Maccabees ii. 13.

sophic writings of the sages, collections of proverbial sayings, works of religious fiction, orations of statesmen, and oracles of mystic seers.

The New Testament is the literature of the Christian Church in its creative epoch; the work still, in the main, of Jewish hands, as Judaism was blossoming into a universal religion. It is thus the literature of the most important religious movement civilization has experienced; a movement whose unspent forces we are feeling still, in the flooding tides of progress. It, too, forms a winnowed library; the siftings of Sayings of Jesus, lives of Christ, apostolical and other letters, visions and romances; and holds the choicest mental products of this fertile era. In it are gathered memoirs of the Founder of Christianity, doctrinal and ethical treatises from the hand of the man who, under Christ, was the chief factor in the early Church; similar essays, in the form of letters, from other more or less important leaders, representing the various phases of original Christianity; a fragmentary and free sketch of the apostolic labors, and the last great effort of apocalyptic genius, in the Revelation of St. John, the Divine.

3. *This literature of the Jewish nation and of the Christian Church is intrinsically noble.*

The Bible has lost much of its fresh charm for us, with whom its finest sayings are household words.

We parsed Virgil and Homer in our boyhood until the aroma of poetry exhaled from their hackneyed pages, and we can scarce think of them now save as grammatical exercises. The Bible has thus palled upon our imagination, through the uninspiring familiarity of early task-work. But were it possible to read it in our manhood for the first time, how the blood would beat and the nerves thrill over some of its pages. We should then understand the sensations of a French *salon* upon a certain occasion. Our shrewd philosopher-minister, Franklin, had previously heard the *literati* wont to gather there ridiculing the Bible, and had guessed that they knew little of it. Upon this evening he observed that he would much like to have the judgment of the assembly on a certain Eastern tale he had lately come across, unknown probably to most of those there present, though long ago translated into their own tongue. Whereupon, drawing from his pocket a copy of the Bible, he had a Parisienne, let into the secret, read in her sweet tones the book of Ruth. The company was thrown into raptures over the charming tale, which lasted until they found its name.

How fresh, with the crisp air of morning, are these tales of primitive tradition! How *naif* these simple stories of Hebrew heroes! What so fine in religious poetry as some of the strains from the Jewish Hymnal? What a noble drama is Job, the Hebrew Faust! How wise the proverbial sayings! What pure passion and lofty imagination stir through the pages of the greater prophets! Where are to be found letters like those of Paul? What biographies have the artless simplicity of the Synoptic Gospels, or the mystic spirituality of the Gospel according to St. John!

No critic of our age has finer literary feeling or more dispassionate judgment than Matthew Arnold; and he has edited the second section of Isaiah as a text book for the culture of the imagination in English schools. In the introduction to this Primer he observes: "What a course of elequence and poetry is the Bible in our schools."

Goethe shared Arnold's love of the Bible, and was so constant a reader of it that his friends reproached him for wasting his time over it. Burke owned his indebtedness to the Bible for his unique eloquence. Webster confessed that he owed to its habitual reading much of his power. Ruskin looks back to the days when a pious aunt compelled him to learn by heart whole chapters of the Bible, for his schooling in the craft of speech, in which he stands unrivaled among living Englishmen.

Emerson writes :

"The most original book in the world is the Bible. This old collection of the ejaculations of love and dread, of the supreme desires and contritions of men, proceeding out of the region of the grand and eternal seems . . . . the alphabet of the nations, and all posterior writings, either the chronicles of facts under very inferior ideas, or when it rises to sentiment, the combinations, analogies, or degradation of this. The elevation of this book may be measured by observing how certainly all observation of thought clothes itself in the words and forms of speech of that book . . . . Whatever is majestically thought in a great moral element, instantly approaches this old Sanscrit . . . . Shakspeare, the first literary genius of the world, the highest in whom the moral is not the predominating element, leans on the Bible ; his poetry presupposes it. If we examine this brilliant influence—Shakspeare—as it lies in our minds, we shall find it reverent, not only of the letter of this book, but of the whole frame of society which stood in Europe upon it, deeply indebted to the traditional morality, in short, compared with the tone of the Prophets, *secondary*. . . . . People imagine that the place which the Bible holds in the world, it owes to miracles. It owes it simply to the fact that it came out of a profounder depth of thought than any other book."[*]

Even what seem to us valueless books turn out, when studied naturally, most interesting and suggestive.

Jonah, that stone of stumbling and rock of offence to the modern youth, becomes, when rightly read, a noble writing, full of the very spirit of our age. Around the tradition of Jonah, the son of Amittai, a prophet of whom we know nothing in other writings, some forgotten author has woven a story, to point a lofty moral. Jonah feels himself called to go to Nineveh and cry against it, because of its wickedness. Quite naturally, he does not relish such an errand.

The prospect of a poor Jew's reforming the gay and dissolute metropolis of the earth, which sat as a queen among the nations, singing to herself,

---

[*] The Dial : October, 1840.

"I will be a lady forever," was not brilliant enough to fascinate him; and the prospect of the reward he would get from the luxurious people of pleasure, whose well-opiated consciences he should rudely rouse by calling their intrigues and carousals wickedness, was only too clear. Jonah fled from his duty. In his flight occurs the marvelous experience with the big fish, that has so troubled dear, pious people who have read as literal history what is plainly legendary. After this fabulous episode, the story takes up its ethical thread. Jonah finds that he cannot flee from the presence of the Lord, that he cannot decline a mission imposed from on high. He goes to Nineveh; cries out against its sins, as God had told him; and, as God had not told him, predicts its overthrow in forty days, as a judgment on its crimes. But, contrary to his expectations, the city is stirred by his preaching; and King and court and people repent and amend their ways. Whereupon the Divine forgiveness is extended at once to these wicked Pagans, and the fate they had deserved is averted. But in this turn of affairs Jonah's prediction failed, and so he was displeased and was very angry, and took the Almighty to task quite roundly, for his lack of vigour.

"Was not this my saying when I was yet in my country? Therefore, I fled before unto Tarshish, for I knew that thou art a gracious God, and merciful, slow to anger, and of great kindness, and repentest thee of the evil."

What was to become of preachers if, after they had threatened destruction upon evil-doers, the Most High went back upon them thus? The later breed of Jonahs may profitably study the after scene, in which God is made to rebuke the frightful selfishness and hardness which, rather than have one's theories belied, would have a city damned.

"Thou hast had pity on the gourd, for the which thou hast not labored. . . . and should not I spare Nineveh, that great city, wherein are more than sixscore thousand persons that cannot discern between their right hand and their left hand, and also much cattle?"

The moral marvel of Nineveh's general repentance on the preaching of an obscure Jew is as unnatural as the physical marvel of the fish story.

Recognizing that the whole tale is a parable, which takes upon it purely legendary drapery, and ridding ourselves thus of all the questions which puzzle Sunday-school scholars and theologians, we are ready to read the meaning of the parable. God is not the God of any one race or religion. He cares for Gentile as for Jew. He sends a prophet of Israel to bid a pagan city repent, that He may forgive it freely. These Pagans understand the message of the Jew. The commands of conscience are owned and honored by the heathen, even more quickly than by the people of God; whose own Jerusalem never thus quickly obeyed a prophet's message. The city whence had come Israel's woes is held up as a pattern to the sacred city herself. All men, then, are brothers, partakers of the same moral and religious nature; children of One Father, whose voice they hear in different tongues, speaking to their souls the same messages of holy love.

Thus read, Jonah becomes the protest of liberal Judaism against the narrow, exclusive tendencies of popular piety in Israel. It is the writing of some genuine Broad-Churchman of the olden time, proclaiming the high truths of Human Brotherhood under a Divine Fatherhood, breathing that spirit of which, long after, another Jew dared say—

"And now abideth faith, hope and charity, but the greatest of these is charity."

If such be the hidden value of one of the least attractive of these writings, we may well say, with Milton,

"I shall wish I may deserve to be reckoned among those who admire and dwell upon them."

4. *This literature has been very influential in the development of progressive civilization.*

When the writings of Greece and Rome had been buried in the ruins of the Roman Empire, the literature of Israel was preserved by the pious care of the Christian Church. The light of Athens went out, and the light of Jerusalem alone illumined the dark ages. The only books known to the mass of men through long centuries were these writings of the Hebrews and the early Christians. Thought was kept alive by them, imagination was fed from them, conscience was educated and vitalized through them. For a thousand years there was practically but one book in Europe—the Bible. When the long gestation of the middle ages was fulfilled, and the modern world was born, while the educated classes read the exhumed classics of Greece, the people still read the Bible. It gave, in the person of Luther, the impulse that restored intellectual liberty and moral health to Europe. It has continued the best read book of Western civilization; the only book much read, until of late, by the mass of men; the one foreign and ancient literature familiar alike to the plain people in Germany and France, in England and America; the common well-spring of inspiration to thought and imagination, to character and conduct.

It is the Magna Charta of our liberties; the revered companion and master of the Pilgrims who sailed the wintry seas, and, on Plymouth Rock, building wiser than they knew, founded a nation covenanting freedom of conscience unto all men; a nation on whose Bell of Independence runs the Bible legend, "Proclaim liberty to the inhabitants thereof."

Wherever society is found to-day in travail with a new and higher order, the conception can be traced to the seminal words of the Bible. The institutions and manners of progressive civilization are what they are because in the heart of that civilization has lain the Bible.

My brothers, were these books nothing more to us than such ancient writings, the literature of so noble a race, a literature intrinsically fine, to which our civilization owes so much of mental and of moral influence, they should win our reverence, and should shame the wantonness of liberalism, falsely so called.

What if in these ancient writings there are ancient errors, the marvels which a child age exaggerated into miracles, stories of savage cruelty and brutal lust in rude, rough times, acts of superstition dark and dreadful, utterances which to us are blasphemous ascribed to the Eternal and Holy One? Such faults are inevitable in the literature that records a nation's growth from barbarism. Were a man in the name of Liberty or in the name of Truth to hunt through Homer, to rake together all the errors and superstitions embalmed in these immortal sagas, to haul up from the obscurity where sensible people leave them the lewdnesses suggested or described, and then to fling these blemishes at the book in which the children of Greece and England and America have read with tingling blood the tales which stirred their souls, by what name would we call him? By that name let him stand forth impaled upon the scorn of an age that has not lost the grace of reverence, who, mindless of majestic age, the dignity of letters, an influence unrivalled and benign, associations tender and most holy, upon these venerable and sacred books spits his shallow scepticism, spumes his spleenful sarcasm, and smuts them with his own sensuality.

Let Irreverence stay her ribald tongue before these illustrious writings, and Indecency vomit her own nastiness elsewhere than on our Bible.

II.

The Bible lays a yet deeper claim upon our reverence. These books constitute the literature of a people whose genius was religion, whose mission was its evolution into universal forms, whose writings express the moods and tenses of that development; whose history is the organic growth which flowered in the life of Him who freed religion from every swathing band, and gave the world its pure essential spirit; after Whom all races are being drawn as one flock under one Shepherd.

1. *Israel's specialty in history was religion.*

Every people finds laid upon it certain necessary activities, in most of which all peoples find their common tasks. Every nation must cultivate agriculture, handicrafts, trade and commerce; must develop social, political and religious institutions. Each people will, however, do some one thing better than the rest of its tasks, better than it is done by other peoples. Each great race has some commanding inspiration; some ideal which masters every other aspiration and ambition, energizes its efforts and shapes its destiny. It creates a specialty among the nations. The real legacy of each great race lies in the works wrought in the line of its highest aptitudes. Thus Rome developed a genius for civil organization. She conquered the whole western world, united isolated nations under one empire, cleared the Mediterranean for safe and free communication, opened roads as arteries through the vast body politic, established post communications for travellers and the mails, carried law and order into every obscure hamlet, consolidated a polity which, by sheer massiveness, lasted for generations after the soul of Rome had fled, and left to posterity, in her institutes, the basis for modern jurisprudence. Thus Greece evolved a genius for art, developed architecture and sculpture to the highest perfection the world has seen, made statues thicker than men in Athens, made men more beautiful than statues, sighed even after Virtue as the Becoming, the Perfect Beauty, left the world temples whose ruins are inspirations, and marbles whose discovery dates the epochs of culture. Israel essayed to do many things that other peoples achieved, and promised success in more than one direction. At a certain period she bade fair to develop into a martial empire, and to become a lesser Assyria or Rome. A little later she seemed about to rival the Phenicians in commerce. About the same time she

"advanced as far as the Greeks before Socrates towards producing an independent science or philosophy." *

But she found herself content with none of these rôles. She had a higher part assigned her in the drama of history, to which her secret instincts resistlessly drew her. Her predominant characteristic was an intense religiousness. Everything in the life of her people took on a serious and devout tone. Patriotism was identified with piety. Her statesmen were reformers, idealists, whose orations were sermons, like the speeches of Gladstone in the Midlothian campaign, dealing with politics in the light of eternal principles. Legislation was developed through the "judgments" of priestly oracles. Poetry lighted her flames at the altar. Philosophy busied itself with ethics. The Muse of History was the Spirit of Holiness. The nation's ambitions were aspirations. Her heroes grew to be saints. The divine became to her, not the true or the beautiful, but the good. She evidently had, as Matthew Arnold said of John Wesley, "a genius for godliness."

2. *Israel's literature became thus a religious literature.*

Her histories were written for edification. They present the past of the people in such light

---

* Ewald: History of Israel, i. 4.

as to inculcate virtue and inspire piety. Her poems are songs of pure love, like Canticles; or dramas whose plot lies in the problem of evil, like Job; or hymns in which the soul seeks communion with God. The Psalter is the hymnal of the temple choir at Jerusalem. The prophets are preachers of righteousness, personal, social, political. Even the writings of her sages or philosophers are almost wholly ethical and religious. No other people's literature is so intensely and pervasively religious. Other nations have religious writings as a part of their general literature. Israel's whole literary life was sacred. There is scarcely a book left by her to which we may not go to feed religion.*

3. *Israel's literature presents us, in the various moods and tenses of her life, with the various phases of religion.*

The glory of a truly National Church is that it takes up into itself every form of spiritual and ethical consciousness within the nation, and exhibits in each successive school of thought, in each movement for a nobler social life, a phase of true religion. This is the glory of Israel. Religion never separated itself into an institution apart from the State.

There was no Jewish Church, of which Dean

---

* Esther is the most notable apparent exception, but this is only apparent.

Stanley wrote the history. Church and State were one. Sacred and secular history flowed in one common stream. The history of Israel was the history of Judaism. Its choicest literature formed its sacred writings. Religion was never narrowed to a theory, an institution, an "ism," a sect, a school. It was as generous and as rich as the broad, free life of the nation. Every factor essential to a noble religion was thus supplied from the sound and healthy life of the people.

The inner life of the soul was voiced in the hymns of Israel, to which we still turn for the inspiration of personal piety in our private devotions; and which lift the public worship of the moderns as they swelled the souls of the hosts who waited in the temple courts at Jerusalem, two thousand years ago.

A cultus of character through ritual and discipline was elaborated by the priesthood in that wonderful system which, rebaptized, does duty still in the Catholic Church. The true outer sphere for personal religion, trained, if need be, by an ecclesiastical cultus, was fashioned by the great prophets, the men of the people; who poured their passion for righteousness into aspirations for a true commonwealth, in which Justice should be throned on law, and international relations be ruled, not by Policy, but by Principle. Natural religion was nobly set forth by the sages in Proverbs, The Wisdom of Jesus, and the other

"Writings;" all of which were characterized by a calm and rational philosophy, that recognized the laws of life and fed the wisdom which obeys them. Even Agnosticism, in so far as it is the confession of the inadequacy of every interpretation of the universe, finds despondent yet still earnest expression in Ecclesiastes, and humble, hopeful expression in Job; and the silence of many of the noblest natures of our age, which the churches brand as irreligious, finds place among the phases of religion in their Sacred Book.*

Almost every form of strenuous ethical life, almost every answer that earnest souls have found to the problem of life, is to be drawn from the writings of this many-sided people. Thus their

---

* In speaking of the book of Esther, Dean Stanley observes that "it never names the name of God from first to last," and remarks: "It is necessary for us that in the rest of the sacred volume the name of God should constantly be brought before us, to show that He is all in all to our moral perfection. But it is expedient for us no less that there should be one book which omits it altogether, to prevent us from attaching to the mere name a reverence which belongs only to the reality. . . . The name of God is *not* there, but the work of God *is*. . . . When Esther nerved herself to enter, at the risk of her life, the presence of Ahasuerus—'I will go in unto the king, and if I perish I perish'—when her patriotic feeling vented itself in that noble cry, 'How can I endure to see the evil that shall come unto my people? or can I endure to see the destruction of my kindred?' —she expressed, although she never named the name of God, a religious devotion as acceptable to Him as that of Moses and David, who, no less sincerely, had the sacred name always on their lips."—*History of the Jewish Church*, iii. 201.

literature feeds a rich and rounded life of religion.

¶ 4. *Israel's literature presents us with the record of a continuous growth of religion upward through its normal stages.*

Religion grows like every form of human life with the growth of man himself. It is coarse, crude and cruel while man is a savage, and as he becomes civilized—by which I mean something more than wealthy—it becomes intelligent, reasonable, ethical and spiritual. The growth of Israel from barbarism carried with this progress the growth of Israel's religion. In the earliest times which we can historically reach the Israelites were semi-nomadic tribes, slightly distinguishable from their kindred Semites. The religion of the people appears to have been then a commingling of fetichism, the worship of things that impressed the imagination, great trees and huge boulders, with the worship of the various powers of nature, the orbs of heaven, the reproductive force of the earth, etc., under the usual savage and sensual symbolisms.

From such unpromising beginnings, through the successive stages of polytheistic idolatries, religion was gradually led up, in the advance of the general life of the people and through the inspirations of a series of great men, to the recognition of One Eternal and infinite Being; the Lord of nature and of man, the Father of all mankind, Holy, Just and Gracious; whose truest worship is the aspirations of his children after goodness.

"Hear, O Israel, the Lord our God is one Lord," writes the Deuteronomist; "and thou shalt love the Lord thy God with all thine heart and with all thy soul and with all thy might."

Malachi, looking round upon the manifold forms of worship of the various nations, and discerning that through them all the soul of man was feeling after one and the same Divine Being, makes God say:

"From the rising of the sun even unto the going down of the same my name is great among the Gentiles; and in every place incense is offered unto me and a pure offering; for my name is great among the heathen, saith the Lord of Hosts."

Micah asks,

"What doth the Lord require of thee, but to do justly, to love mercy and to walk humbly with thy God?"

Of this continuous growth of religion the Old Testament is the record.

5. *Israel's literature records the forcing forward of this growth of religion, as by some Power back of man, shaping its ends, rough-hew them as it might.*

The Niebuhr of Hebrew history rightly pointed out this significant fact in the introduction to his great work.

"The manifold changes and even confusions and perversities, which manifest themselves in the long course of the threads of its history, ultimately tend to the solution of this great problem."—Ewald: Intro.

A singular succession of great men arise to save and revive and reform religion in every critical epoch. Moses, Samuel, Elijah, Isaiah, Jeremiah, Ezekiel, Ezra, Judas Maccabeus come upon the stage, one after the other, perform their several parts with singular aptitude, and prepare the way for the next movement when it comes due. The history of the people rightly read becomes a mighty drama, in which the right man is never wanting at the right time, and the action moves on steadily toward a climax.

The experiences of the people, even those most perplexing to the faith of the nation at the time, fit singularly into this organic evolution of religion. The rending of the Kingdom of David, that blighted the fair prospect of a martial empire, turned the nation aside from the false career on which it was entering. The overthrow of the Northern and then of the Southern Kingdom, and the deportation of the people to Babylonia, seemingly the ruin of the sister countries, threw them in upon their inner life; and in the exile their religion found its highest reach of thought.

Even that hierarchical movement which so quickly followed upon this bloom of prophetism, and which to the superficial look seems only the arrest of life and the beginning of death, reveals a legitimate function in the organic processes of the national religion. In this priestly organization of institutional religion, all free prophetic inspiration did indeed die out for over four centuries. But even this was a necessity for the right flowering of religion. The age was not ready, politically or intellectually, for the ripening of the thoughts of the prophets. Had they ripened then, they would have fallen to the ground, as the untimely fruit of a too-early spring. Four centuries were to be tided over before the political and intellectual conditions were found for the blossoming of this flower. This holding back of the normal evolution of Hebraism was the function of the Priestly Reaction—a curious parallel to the function of Catholicism in Mediæval Christianity.

Like the Catholic Church, the Jewish priesthood held society together when, in the destruction of the political power, there was no other bond of unity. As in the Catholic Church, the High Priest became a temporal ruler, the Prince of Israel, as he was called; and kept the sacred city still the seat of government. As in Catholicism, the institutionalizing of religion that followed the period of free prophetic life was an effort to embody that life, to incrust and thus preserve it; and, in the one case as in the other, though the crust of institutions choked the further growth of spiritual religion, it yet did keep it sluggishly alive within this hard bark, through times that else would have proved fatal to it. As in Catholicism, this priestly cultus really drilled deep into the natures of men the principles and laws and habitudes of ethical and spiritual religion; and stored the force which, when its rigid routine and fettering formalism became unbearable, burst through this crust and opened a new world of fresh, free life.

Of this singular shaping of the nation's experiences to further the growth of true religion, the Old Testament is the impressive record.

6. *Israel's literature thus presents the picture of a nation's patient, insistent pressing forward, through long centuries, toward the fruition of its ideal, the realization of true religion.*

So continuous is Israel's movement toward the ideal of religion, so straight the line of her advance, that it seems as though the nation had a conscious aim, seen afar and steadfastly pursued by generation after generation, unwilling to stop short of attainment. It is the founder of scientific Biblical criticism who thus expresses his sense of the wonderfulness of this historic movement:

"This aim is Perfect Religion; a good which all aspiring nations of antiquity made an attempt to attain; which some, the Indians and Persians, for example, really labored to achieve with admirable devotion of noble energies, but which this people alone clearly discerned from the beginning, and then pursued for centuries through all difficulties, and with the utmost firmness and consistency, until they attained it, so far as among men and in ancient times attainment was possible."*

---

* Ewald : History of Israel, i. 4.

7. *The literature of Christian Israel records the realization of this long sought ideal, the fruition of this organic growth.*

The nation found the times ripe at last for the final process of this historic evolution; the dead cerements of Judaism fell apart, and thereout bloomed that perfect flower of religion, the religion of the Christ, simple, free, ethical, spiritual. The extant literature of this last creative effort of Israel constitutes the New Testament. The Gospels tell the story of the life of the Founder of Christianity, clearly enough in the main outlines, and embalm many of the words and deeds of the Son of Man. The other writings of the New Testament illustrate the working of the thought and spirit of the Christ in the Church bodying around Him through the growth of a century. In them we see that the long cherished ideal of Israel, an Ethical and Universal Religion, had at last incarnated itself in The Master whose plans laid the foundation of this new Order; into which men were coming from the east and from the west, and from the north and from the south, and were sitting down in the Kingdom of God.

The high-water mark of religion in human history is recorded in these writings. To enter into the spirit of these writings is to feel the force of the free, full tides of ethical and spiritual life which rose, as never before nor since, in the dawning day of Christianity. The flow of such a force within the individual soul and through society has been the power of the New Testament in Christendom.

8. *This organic growth of a national religion into a catholic ideal, not without parallels elsewhere, is, however, unique in respect to the conditions for a truly Universal Religion.*

The scene of this evolution is not the heart of the East, as in Buddhism, but the meeting point of East and West. Palestine is the race centre of the earth. Camels unload in Jerusalem the goods laden upon them in the seats of the most ancient empires; and on her pebbly beaches the Mediterranean rolls, bearing the commerce of Europe. Behind Judea lies the past, before it opens the future. Its Race-Man came at the epoch when, first in history, the East and West were brought together under one empire and opened to the free interchange of thought. And when we analyze the religion of the Christ, grown in this central land and coming to the birth in this central period, we find that it holds, alone on earth, the elements of each race-religion in well proportioned combination.

No eastern religion, Buddhism not excepted, appears to contain conceptions that satisfy the western mind. The religion of the Christ, however, can be shown to hold whatever ideas and ideals make vital the great race-religions of the

East. It is as many sided as humanity, and presents a family face to every people. It takes up the ideas and ideals of other religions, disengages and deposits whatever in them is temporal and circumstantial, preserves whatever is essential and eternal in them, combines these vital elements with the polar truths needful to their wholesomeness, and crystallizes ethical and spiritual religion into perfect forms, forms capable of translation into the idioms of every race of earth. This religion of the Christ is the one religion which today holds the promise and potency of further evolution, in the progressive civilization of mankind on which it is enthroned.

9. *Of the literature of the people through whom came this organic evolution of the keystoning religion of earth what can we say but that it records a real revelation, coming through genuine personal inspirations from on high!*

Revelation is the opposite aspect of the mystery which we call discovery; the uncovering of that which was hidden; the unveiling of that which was not known; the coming on of truth into the light wherein man can see it. "Discovery" expresses the human effort by which truth is thus uncovered and found out. "Revelation" expresses the divine effort which lies back of all human aspirations and endeavors; as the Spirit within man stirs him up to seek for Truth, flashes in upon his mind strange hints of where and how she is to be found, allures him onward with the mystic whispers of her voice, until at length he stands upon the mount of vision whence her holy form is seen, and cries—"I have found her!"

To him who believes in a Spirit of Truth, guiding men into all truth, the growth of ethical and spiritual religion into perfect form in Jesus Christ is a real revelation. It is the oncoming of the Light which lighteth every man that is in the world; the dawning of the day of earth on the hills of Judea, over which has risen the Sun of Righteousness with healing in His wings.

This revelation came not to the mystic "man writ large" we call society, direct from heaven in abstract form. It came to individual men, struggling for larger light and nobler life, and breathing their higher spirit on their fellows. Religion is always *life*, the experience of *souls*. We can name the individuals through whom each important advance was made. The greater souls who led the worship of the host welcoming the rising Light, thrilled with the vibrations of a voice deeper and holier than the voice of man. The lesser souls who formed the chorus of this anthem of The Dawn thrilled each alike with this mystic sense of God. That which we must aver of every truth discovered or revealed, of every knowledge needful to man and won by man; that which we must affirm as the only rational interpretation of the mysterious suggestions rising below the conscious thoughts of man, and prompting to noblest benedictions on the race; that we must, with deepened awe, say of the holiest truths shown to the human soul,—Inspired!

With sincere and reverent confession we must say then in the words of Holy Writ:

"Holy men of God spake as they were moved by the Holy Ghost." "Every Scripture profitable for teaching, for reproof, for correction, for instruction in righteousness is God-inspired." *

The consciousness and experience of Israel could not have found fitter expression than in the words of our great seer:

"I conceive a man as always spoken to from behind, and unable to turn his head and see the speaker. In all the millions who have head the voice, none ever saw the face. That well-known voice speaks in all languages, governs all men; and none ever caught a glimpse of its form. If the man will exactly obey it, it will adopt him, so that he shall not any longer separate it from himself in his thought; he shall seem to be it, he shall be it. If he listen with insatiable ears, richer and greater wisdom is taught him, the sound swells to a ravishing music, he is borne away as with a flood, he is the fool of ideas, and leads a heavenly life. But if his eye is set on the things to be done, and not on the truth that is still taught, and for the sake of which the things

---

* The Old Testament is a record of the growth of human intelligence in relation to the Deity—of the revelation made by Spirit to spirit. When therefore God is described as *speaking* to man, he does so in the only way in which He who is a Spirit can speak to one encompassed with flesh and blood; not to the outward organs of sensation, but to that intelligence which is kindred to Himself the great Fountain of knowledge.—DAVIDSON: *Introduction to the Old Testament*, i. 233.

are to be done, then the voice grows faint, and at last is but a humming in his ears." *

We have thus seen in the Bible an ancient and noble literature, the literature of a noble race, the literature supremely influencing and enriching Christian civilization; demanding, therefore, our rational reverence, as constituting a truly Sacred Book.

We have seen in the Old Testament the literature of the people of religion, commissioned with its normal evolution; writings charged with deep religiousness; the records of the various moods and tenses through which religion grew continuously and insistently toward perfection, in an organic process watched and directed by a Higher Power than man. We have seen in the New Testament the record of the realization of this long-sought aim of the people of religion; the story of the Divine Man, who breathed religion out into perfection, and the writings that depict the bodying around Him of the Universal Church, the Church in whose truth and life is growing the religion of the future, "the Christ that is to be."

The fuller knowledge of our age, in evanishing the unreal Bible restores the real Bible. It is the record of the visioning and embodiment of the Human Ideal, the Divine Image—The Christ. It is the Providentially prepared Hand Book of religion, in whose rich and varied phases of ethical

---

* Emerson: Miscellanies, p. 200.

and spiritual thought all men may find the nourishment they need. It is the spiritual reality our fathers rightly felt, but wrongly expressed, when they called it as a whole The Word of God. It holds the words proceeding from out of the mouth of God on which man liveth. It bodies in "letters" The Word of God, embodied in the flesh in Jesus Christ the Lord. It records a real revelation. This revelation, however, denies no other revelation. It affirms the fact of the withdrawal of a veil in each new knowledge won; the fact that man has felt in calling the new knowledge a discovery; and it interprets this unveiling as Tennyson has learned of it to do:

"And out of darkness come the hands
That reach through nature, moulding man."

These books are the products of a real inspiration. This inspiration, however, denies no other inspiration. It interprets the sense of a higher than human influence in the noblest searchers after truth, throughout the world, in every action of the intellect. It affirms the validity of that consciousness.*

The revelation in the Bible is the Light of God

---

* "To hear people speak," said Goethe, "one would almost believe that they were of opinion that God had withdrawn into silence since those old times, and that man was now placed quite upon his own feet, and had to see how he could get on without God and his daily invisible breath."—CONVERSATIONS, *March* 11, 1832.

which streams through it, making it a "lamp unto our feet." The inspiration in the Bible is the life of God breathing through it into man, "and he becomes a living soul." The book which, above all others, reveals God to man, he must call the supreme revelation of God. The book which, above all others, inspires the life of God in man, he must call the most inspired of God.

If, then, any one asks me how he may know that there is a revelation in the Bible, I tell him to walk in its light, and see what it reveals. If any one asks me how I know that the Bible is inspired, I answer him in Mr. Moody's words:

"I know that the Bible is inspired, because it 'inspires me.'"

III.

The wrong use of the Bible.

"God, then, is quite simple and true, both in word and deed; neither is He changed Himself, nor does He deceive others— neither by visions, nor discourses, nor the pomp of signs. * * * * When any one alleges such things as these about the gods, we must show disapproval, and not grant them the privilege of a chorus; neither should we suffer teachers to employ them in the training of youth—if, at least, our guardians are to be pious and divine men."

PLATO: The Republic; Book II.

"This, it seems, is the modern method of coming to inquire of the oracles of God; by this process they become a light to our feet, a lamp to our path! Accept the book as a whole, and then treat all the portions of it just as you like. Confess all its words to be the words of the Lord, and then you may yourself be lords over them, and may perform moral miracles by turning the bread of life into stones for casting at your enemies."

MAURICE: What is Revelation, p. 475.

III.

The wrong use of the Bible.

Every Scripture inspired of God is also profitable for teaching, for reproof, for correction, for instruction in righteousness.—2 Timothy, iii., 16.

THE Unreal Bible is fading upon the vision of our age. You have probably all perceived this more or less clearly. I have uttered the conviction which many of you have held in secret with misgivings and self-reproaches, and have shown you some of the many reasons why, as it seems to me, this view can no longer be held by men of open minds. The Real Bible is as yet vaguely seen, and, therefore, its power is feebly felt. According to their natures men are indulging in flippant flings at a vanished superstition, or grieving silently over the disappearance of the ancient light which ruled the night of earth. I have sought to clear your vision of the new moon rising upon us, the same holy light God set in the heavens of old, though changed in the altered atmosphere of earth.

I propose now to translate the generalities of the previous sermons into some practical applications. I want to-day to make more distinct certain wrong uses of the Bible which grow out of the old view of it; wrong uses from which great mischiefs have come to the cause of true religion, and great trouble to individual souls; abuses which fall away in the light of a more reasonable understanding of the Bible. The Bible viewed as a book let down from heaven, whose real "author" is God, as the Westminster Catechism affirmed; a book dictated to chosen penman and written out by their amanuenses under a direction which secured them against error on every subject of which they treated; a book thus given to the world to be an authoratitive and infallible oracle for human information on all the great problems of life—naturally calls for uses which, apart from this theory, are gross and superstitious abuses.

I.

It is a wrong use of the Bible to set it in its entirety before all classes and all ages.

On the old view of the Bible no man might dare to omit portions of it in public reading or home instruction. The horrible atrocities and brutal lusts of the early Hebrews, and the coarsenesses of their later days, as unbearable by modern ears as the rough talk of Shakespeare's ladies, had all to be read to mixed assemblies of young men and maidens; and be read with blushing face by the pure mother to the purer children at her knees. For us, who see the Bible in its true light, there is no necessity for a minister to offend against the taste of a refined age, or for a mother to introduce the unsoiled soul of her child to evil, by reading straight through the successive chapters of the Bible. It has been left for Protestant piety to excel Romanists and Jews in superstition. The Church of Rome, as you know, discourages the use of the Bible by her laity, erring in the other extreme. The Jewish rabbis had a saying that no one should read the Canticles before he was thirty years of age. If you follow the public readings of the Bible in this church from your own Bibles, you must often appreciate the relief this liberty of omission brings. Use the Bible in this way with your children at home. Who would think of an indiscriminate use of the original Shakespeare? Stage managers cut him so freely for rendering before grown up folk as to have made another Shakespeare. He who cares for his children's innocence will set before them an expurgated edition, like that of Rolfe. So we should use at home such an expurgated edition of the Scriptures as "The Child's Bible," published by Cassel, Petter & Galpin, of London. No timid soul need fear that imprecation in the last chapter of the Revelation :

> If any man shall take away from the words of the book of this prophecy God shall take away his part out of the book of life.

That sounds like the ruling passion, strong in death, of the Son of Thunder, who in youth asked if he should call down fire from heaven upon a hamlet which did not welcome Jesus, and was well rebuked for his zeal by the gracious Master. It is part of the human weakness through which the voice of God speaks, taking its tone from the defects of the instrument. This imprecation had reference, in all probability, solely to the copyists, against whose carelessness the author sought to guard himself by an awful threat. It certainly had reference to this book alone. Not until long afterwards did the Church determine what books were to enter the canon of the New Testament, and in what order they were to stand. That order placed the Revelation as the last book in the canon, and thus made this threat appear to cover the whole Bible.*

---

* Our advancing knowledge of the early portions of the Bible is clearing its offensive portions of the grossness which characterized them as literal histories, by resolving them into nature-myths, or into social traditions, symbolical stories of casuistry, "token-tales," whose original meaning had been lost by the time they were committed to writing.

Every school-boy knows how the worst stories of the Greek gods and goddesses lose their immorality as seen to be parables of nature's processes, myths, whose poetry had exhaled in the course of time. Goldziher's "Mythology Among the Hebrews," shows the mythic character of many of these revolting Jewish stories, though his theory carries him off his feet. "Fenton's "Early Hebrew Life," brings out the social and casuistical origin of many of these traditions as decisions, "Judgments,"

II.

It is a wrong use of the Bible to accept its utterances indiscriminately as the words of God, to quote every saying of every speaker in its pages, or every deed of every actor in its histories as expressing to us the mind of God.

Such use of the Bible is thoughtlessly common. Some time ago before going into a church in

of the village elders and priests upon cases of conduct, thrown into the form of imaginary stories to make them realistic and ensure their preservation. "In this way, various dubious points of primitive morality and politics were governed; and the stories which enshrine them stand to primitive life in much the same relation as do collections of precedents to modern lawyers, and dictionaries of cases of conscience to father confessors." (p. 81)

But, as these aspects of such traditions as Lot and his daughters, Judah and Tamar, &c., cannot be divined without interpretation, they should be omitted from our children's Bibles.

My suggestion of an expurgated Bible, on which so many hard criticisms have been passed, seemed to me innocent enough, since most sensible people have been in the habit of expurgating the Bible for themselves, in home readings and in the readings in the churches. This is what Plato thought of such stories in the sacred book of the Grecians:

"Whatever beautiful fable they may invent, we should select, and what is not so, we should reject: and we are to prevail on nurses and mothers to repeat to the children such fables as are selected, and fashion their minds by fables * * * For though these things were true, yet I think they should not be so readily told to the unwise and the young, but rather concealed from them. As little ought we to describe in fables, the battles of the giants and other many and various feuds, both of gods and heroes, with their own kindred and relatives; but if we would persuade them that never at all should one citizen hate another, and that it is not holy, such things as these are rather to be told them in early childhood; and the poets should be obliged to compose consistently with these views * * * Young persons are not able to judge what is allegory and what is not, but whatever opinions they receive at such an age are wont to be obliterated with difficulty, and immovable. Hence one would think, we should of all things endeavor, that what they should first hear be composed in the best manner for exciting them to virtue."

"Republic," Book II.

whose service I was asked to participate, I ventured to show some slight hesitancy in using certain Psalms which were set down in the Psalter for the day. When asked, why, I mildly answered that I could not request a Christian congregation to join with me in singing, after the embittered Jews in Babylon:

> Remember, O Lord, the children of Edom, in the day of Jerusalem. How they said, "Down with it! down with it! even to the ground.' Oh, daughter of Babylon, who art to be wasted, Happy shall he be that rewardeth thee as thou hast served us. Happy shall he be that taketh thy little ones and throweth them against the stones.

Nor could I ask the people to unite in praying:

> Make their nobles like Oreb and Zeeb; yea, all their princes as Zeba and Salmana.

I had in mind the fate of Oreb and Zeeb and of Zeba and Salmana, splendidly brave fellows even in their death, as told in the seventh and eighth chapters of Judges, where you can learn what sort of prayer was this of those savage Jews. Naturally, as I thought, I objected to voicing such heathen imprecations in the nineteenth century of the era of the Prince of Peace. My good friend, with a look of amazement, replied, "Why, these Psalms are in the Bible." That ended the question for him.

This incident is typical of a vast quantity of wrong uses of the Bible. Thus our American slaveholder read that 'precious' word of the ancient tradition, "Cursed be Ham," and smoothed his troubled conscience. He had the sanction of the Bible for the curse plainly upon Africa. He was fulfilling the Divine will in breeding black cattle for the auction block. Piety and profit were one, and godliness had great gain, and some contentment also. Thus the extermination of the Canaanites, for which the Hebrews pleaded long after the Divine order, and for which they had substantial warrant in Destiny's determination to rid the land of these corrupting tribes and make room for the noble life Israel was to develop, has been the stock argument of kings and soldiers for their bloody trade. Thus poor human consciences have been sorely hurt and troubled as men have read, in stories such as those of Jael and Sisera and Jacob and Esau, of acts which their better nature instinctively condemned. They have felt themselves arraigning the Bible and suspecting God.

If indeed the Bible is a book let down from the skies, of which God can be called the 'author,' then all such uses of it may be correct enough, and in those dark and savage words and deeds I may be obliged to find the words of God and the deeds He holds up to our admiration and imitation; though I do not see that such a use is a necessity, even on this theory. Fancy a man quoting Shylock when he pleads for his bond, or Iago's devilish innuendos against Ophelia's purity, as showing what Shakespeare liked or what he would have us imitate! "These are the words of Shakespeare!" Yes, but of Shakespeare's Shylock, Shakespeare's Iago.

If, however, the Old Testament is the national

library of the Jews, I must expect to find all sorts of early Jewish notions, in ethics and religion, bodied in the words of the speakers they introduce, and the deeds of the men of whom they tell the tales.

If the Bible is the record of a real revelation which came in the spirits of ancient men, through the historic growth of conscience and reason; and if these books are the literature embalming that growth of a people out of ignorance and superstition into the light of pure ethics and spiritual religion; then I must look to find all sorts of crudities and crassnesses in the representation of God, and all phases of unmoral and immoral life, as parts of the error and imperfection out of which they were educated. These deeds and words are the milestones in the path of progress by which Judaism reached Christianity. If the individual is to reproduce the story of the race, as our wise men tell us, then these words and deeds are in the Bible to carry us through the same course of education; to exercise our consciences in discriminating right from wrong, and to lead us to grow out of such conceptions and desires toward the spirit of Christ. In a cruise last summer we dropped anchor in a lovely little out-of-the-way harbor of Buzzard's Bay, which proved to be near Pocasset; where, not long ago, a pious man, reading the Hebrew tradition of Abraham and Isaac, as a real command of the Most High, and having this word of the Lord borne in on his mind, as spoken to himself, murdered his child in sacrifice to God—no angel interfering to stay his knife. He simply made a *reductio ad absurdum* of this use of the Bible.*

III.

It is a wrong use of the Bible to accept everything recorded therein as necessarily true.

If the historians were simply the amanuenses of the Infinite Spirit, then of course they could not have erred in anything they recorded. If they were ordinary writers, trying to tell the story of their peoples' growth; searching court archives, state annals, old parchments of forgotten writers, consulting the traditions of town and village, using their material in the best way their abilities enabled them to do; using all to teach virtue and religion, for which alone they were specially qualified of God; then all questions of historical accuracy are beside the mark. Nothing in their inspiration guarantees their historical accuracy; their philological learning in using ancient poetic language, or their critical judgment in detecting

---

* How then are we to know what words and deeds express the mind of God, are words of the Lord, examples He presents for our imitation? By the mind of God manifest in 'the express image of His person?' All morality and religion is to be tried by 'the mind which was in Christ,' 'the spirit of Christ which dwelleth in us.'

exaggerations. Are we to wait anxiously upon the latest Assyrian tablets or the freshest Egyptian mummy to confirm our faith that God has spoken to the spirit of man? Are we to quake in our shoes when a few ciphers are cut off from the roll of Israel's impossible armies? If much that we read as literal history turns out legend and myth, are we to find a painful alternative between a blind credulity and as blind a skepticism? We follow this same re-reading of Roman and Grecian story untroubled, and see the heroes of our childhood turn into races and sun-myths without calling the Muse of History a fraud.

Has it been such comfort to us to read the doings of Samson as actual history, slaying a thousand men with the jawbone of an ass, tying fire-brands to the tails of three hundred foxes, etc., that we should resent the translation of this impossible hero into the Semitic Hercules, a solar myth? Or if, perchance, the historian accepted from remote antiquity the accounts of great deeds and striking events, as they were told at the camp fires of the Hebrew nomads, or in the merry makings of the Palestinian villages, with an ever growing nimbus of the marvelous gathering around them; and if thus impossible marvels are reported to us soberly, are we to be compelled to accept them uncritically or reject the Bible altogether? The Bible itself points us to the interpretation of such legends. We have some histories written by the actors in the scenes narrated. Nehemiah and Ezra, leaders in the most important movement of Hebrew history after the migration led by Moses, left accounts of their work from their own pens. In such a crucial epoch as that of the restoration of the Jews to their native land, after the dispersion in Babylonia, we might expect to find miraculous interpositions on behalf of the chosen people, if they are to be found anywhere. But no tale of miracle adorns their simple pages. No other Old Testament history, written by the actors in its scenes, tells of miracles. Such stories are found in the traditions written down long after the events narrated, by men who knew nothing of the facts at first hand. Exceptions to this rule occur alone in such startling events as the mysterious calamity that befell Sennacherib; which strongly impressed the imagination of the people and naturally gave rise to exaggerations that we can no longer resolve.

Perhaps Elisha's iron axe head did swim upon the water. I am prepared to believe almost anything after our spiritualistic mediums, and their exposers. Whether it did or did not concerns me no whit. I shrug my shoulders and read on. I cannot make out the historical fact which was at the basis of the Red Sea deliverance; nor do I care much to make out this or any other Old Testament miracle. If I felt obliged to accept literally these stories, or to lose my faith in the voice of God which speaks through the men of the Bible I should care greatly.

In the true view of the Bible I am delivered from solicitude about these traditions, and am under no constraint of credulity. Those who can believe the story of Elisha and the bears, or of Elijah's ascension into heaven, may; those who cannot, need not; and both alike should reverently read their Bibles, not for these tales of wonder, but for the still small voice of the eternal spirit sounding through holy lives and holier aspirations, until He came whose life was the Word of God, the Wonderful.*

IV.

It is a wrong use of the Bible to consult it as a heathen oracle for the determining of our judgments and the decision of our actions.

The pagans, even such grand old pagans as the Romans, before undertaking any important action would solemnly consult the auspices. Men with rea-

---

*In what is said above there is no positive denial intended of the Old Testament miracles. We are in no position to deny them. The point is simply that they are not bounden on us in any reasonable and reverent recognition of a real historical revelation in the Old Testament, and need trouble no one who cannot receive them. The miracles of Christ, when reduced to the wonders reported by the conjoint testimony of the synoptics,—*i.e.*, to the common tradition of the early church, stand apart from all other Scripture miracles; having a reasonable and natural character as the powers of such a personality, and coming within the ken of our visions of possibility. They are imaged in the well attested powers of rare men. They appear as in no wise violations of law, but as the manifestations of nature's laws and forces worked by the normal man, having 'dominion' over the earth. "The wise soul expels disease."

son given them of God would stand anxiously around the steaming entrails of a bird, to find out whether the fates were propitious to their undertaking. Great generals would open or delay a campaign according to the intestinal revelations of a goose. Intelligent people use the Bible in some such way. When at a loss how to proceed, instead of calmly consulting their own judgments and the judgments of their wisest friends, and then acting like reasonable beings, men and women will open their Bibles at random, let their eyes rest on the first verse which arrests their attention, and accept any possible bearing on the question in hand as the voice of God. The journals of John Wesley and other eminent men contain examples of this abuse of the Bible. I call it an abuse, for such action degrades the Bible to the level of a heathen oracle. Isaiah, like all the great prophets, habitually contrasted the true and the false communications of of the Divine will by the test of the reasonableness of their manifestations. The real prophet heard the voice of God, not so much in dreams and visions, in the "peepings and chirpings" of the oracles, as in the calm and sober working of his mind, illumined from on high. The oracle was the antithesis of the prophet. The oracle represented unintelligent, unreasonable, magical means of getting at a desired knowledge. The prophet represented the intelligent, reasoning, natural means of getting at that knowledge; the lighting of that candle of the Lord which is the spirit of man. In the profound double significance of the original, the *Logos* is the Word or the Reason. The Word of God which comes to man is the Divine Reason, of which each human reason is a ray. To train and use that reason in all our exigencies, humbly looking up to the Eternal Reason to let the light in us be pure and clear, is the way to hear the Word of God.

To consult the reason of the holy men of old on themes whereon they were qualified to speak is rational and right. To make of their writings a new oracle whose mysterious meanings we are to guess, as the ancient Greeks puzzled over the messages of the Delphic shrine, is to revive Paganism in Christianity. "No prophecy is of any private interpretation." No passage in the Bible was written, centuries ago, with reference to your private affairs. All that is there written concerned men and affairs of distant days. The principles there applied will help you now, if you will take the trouble to search for them, since principles do not change with the fashions.

v.

It is a wrong use of the Bible to go to it, as the heathen went to their oracles, for divination of the future.

The pagan oracles were the shrines of a Power sought for the forecasting of events. The inspiration of an oracle was proven by the success of its predictions. In the same way men have turned to the Bible as a sort of sacred weather bureau, a book which, if we could only interpret its mystic utterances, would tell us what things were going to happen upon the earth. I remember an eloquent Irish divine who came to this country on a great mission a number of years ago. His first sermon was on Ezekiel's vision by the Chebar. He said that this was the age of science, and that such a marvel as science could not have escaped the vision of the prophets. This mystic creature which the prophet saw, with wheels, whose appearance was like burning coals of fire, which turned not as it went, and so on, was—the locomotive! This folly was only more undisguised than the mass of the lucubrations called Prophetic Studies.

Let any political crisis occur, and some sage will write a book showing how Daniel had foretold this issue of diplomacy. I have not forgotten the learned tracts and essays called forth by the fascination Louis Napoleon exercised upon the imaginations of half-educated people; all proving beyond a doubt that he was the mystic man of sin, the Anti-Christ in whom history was to culminate.

America, the restoration of the Jews to Palestine, and the Church of Rome especially inspire, at present, these crazy conjectures. They ought all to issue from Bedlam.

This mad and maddening use of what, rightly read, are noble and instructive books, grows out of a misunderstanding of what were the functions of Hebrew prophecy.

Prophecy has been taken as a synonyme for prediction. There is not much verbal difference between foretelling and forthtelling, but there is a vast difference for the purposes of religion. Taking prophecy as the synonyme of foretelling, the essential function of the prophets became predicting. They were supposed to have been busy in forecasting the things which should come to pass in the far future. The success of these long-range predictions was the demonstration of their being charged with miraculous powers. The prophecies constituted the chief evidence for the supernatural character of the Bible. Of course, with this theory in the mind of the church, a predictive character would be read into everything capable of bearing it; and the history of the Hebrews, the eloquent orations of their great statesmen, the pious longings of their hymn writers, became mystic anticipations of everything in the heavens above and the earth beneath.

But Hebrew prophecy never was the synonyme for prediction. It meant forth-telling. The prophets were "men of the spirit," whose pure nature mirrored the supreme laws of earth, the moral laws; whose intuitions made application of those laws to the policies of statecraft, and enabled them to divine the issues of the stirring events amid which they lived. Their glory is that they saw above the brute force of great empires the might of right, and dared to vision its triumph, and that history has verified their moral insight. But they chiefly spake, as the author of The Revelation declares of his prophecy, "of things which must shortly come to pass" upon the earth. Their horizon bounded a very nigh future; the approach of Syrian, Assyrian, Egyptian invaders, the overthrow of Jerusalem, etc.

In these predictions they were often mistaken; nearly as often in error as in the right. We seldom hear of these unfulfilled prophecies, but they are in your Bibles. They should teach you, that which the prophets tried so hard to teach their own cotemporaries, that the essential distinction of the true prophet was not that he predicted the future, for this they scornfully left to the false prophets, the oracles of the pagan Jews, but that they forthtold the inner mind and will of God, read the 'laws mighty and brazen' which constitute the essential nature of the Most High and hold the supreme felicity of man. I believe I know of no one passage of the prophets which can be certainly said to point to any event beyond the near future of the writer. Only in so far as they spoke of the ideal forces, of ethical victories, did they launch out upon the far future.

But you say, Do not the Old Testament prophets surely point on to Christ? I answer both No, and Yes. Of any mere literal prediction of the events of His life I know none. The many passages that have been made to read like predictions of His miraculous birth, His sale for thirty pieces of silver, and so on, refer to personages and experiences in the time of the writers. Isaiah expressly says this about the Virgin—that is, the young bride— who was to conceive and bear a son. Before he should be able to distinguish right from wrong the relief of Jehovah to Israel would appear. The passages which seem to our eyes, looking through orthodox spectacles, to have this predictive character, lose it in a more exact translation.

It is doubtless true that the Gospels make many such applications of Old Testament words, adding to their record of minute incidents—" That it might be fulfilled which was spoken by........saying." But the Gospels, as we now possess them, have been slowly fashioned by the labor of many hands, working over the tradition which gradually shaped itself out of the reminiscences of multitudes of men and women. Pious Jews, trained in this Rabbinical use of their Sacred Scriptures, delighting to make application of ancient mystic sayings to the life of their adorable Messiah, read into the Gospel narrative these fulfillments of prediction.

This use of the Old Testament has been pushed

to absurdity in learned books over which I have patiently toiled. "The Gospel of Leviticus," gave me the Hebrew civic and ecclesiastic legislation mystified into 'sound evangelical' symbols. "Christ in the Psalms" twisted every heathenish imprecation of the Hebrew hymns into language which could be put upon the lips of the dear Lord, and turned the bitterest curses into sweet and gracious benedictions.

The culmination of this moon-struck exegesis, as far as my knowledge reaches, is in the ancient and fantastic reading of the tradition of the escape of the spies from Jericho, which gave a young and eloquent Bishop of our church a favorite sermon; wherein he showed conclusively that the scarlet cord by which Rahab let down her visitors over the city wall was a type of the atoning blood of Christ!

This Chinese puzzle-book of predictions exists nowhere save in the imagination of its readers.

There was, however, a most real and substantial typifying of Christ through the Old Testament; but it was natural, organic, ethical and spiritual; in those books as first in the lives of the people. The growth of the nation onward toward the true Image of God, the true Human Ideal; the travail of the nation with the Divine-Human Character which at the last came to the birth in Jesus the Christ; this was a mystery of natural, organic evolution, which 'must give us pause' in every shallow denial of a supernatural involution in human history. This makes true rationalism reverent before 'that Holy Thing' born not alone of Mary but of Mary's race, begotten plainly of the overshadowings of some Holy Ghost, of whom our best judgment is, now as of old,— "He shall be called the Son of the Highest."

The whole history of Israel is a growth of The Christ, and that is the abiding wonder of it.

In such a mystic evolution it may well be, in history as in nature, that the organic processes type the oncoming form of life; but to trace these rightly there is needed a finer criticism than that which has given us the orthodox typology.*

Let us pause here for to-day. And let us take home, as the heart-thought of the morning, an assurance which may comfort us as we stand under the shadow of Christmas. If the dear Christ's throne stood on any such flimsy basis of prophecy as men have built up beneath it, then, when the underpinnings came tumbling out, as to-day they are doing, we might fear that His authority was dropping in

---

* So judicious a commentator as Dean Alford, in his introduction to the Second Epistle to the Thessalonians, discussing the vexed question of the Daniel-like section in the third chapter, so wholly unlike Paul observes:

"If we have" (in any sense, God speaking in the Bible) "then, of all "passages, it is in these, which treat so confidently of futurity, that "we must recognize His voice; if we have it not in these passages, "then, *where are we to listen for it at all?*"—Greek Testament III:64.

with them; that no longer we were to call Him Master and King; that criticism had pronounced His *decheance*. But His throne really rests on a nation's growth of the human Ideal and Divine Image. And, since this nation's growth was on the same general lines as the religious and ethical progress of other races, His throne rests on no less secure a foundation than humanity's evolution of the human Ideal and Divine Image. Man's best and noblest life aspires after an ideal which is the Christly character. Man's best and noblest thoughts of God fashion a vision which is the God revealed in Christ. He is Humanity's " Master of Life."

IV.

The wrong use of the Bible.

"The Scriptures will be more studied than they have been, and in a different manner—not as a magazine of propositions and mere dialectic entities, but as inspirations and poetic forms of life; requiring, also, divine inbreathings and exaltations in us, that we may ascend into their meaning. No false *precision*, which the nature and conditions of spiritual truth forbid, will, by cutting up the body of truth into definite and dead morsels, throw us into states of excision and division, equally manifold. We shall receive the truth of God in a more organic and organific manner, as being itself an essentially vital power."

    HORACE BUSHNELL: God in Christ; p. 93.

"But, further, the zealots for the Bible *as it is*, just because it *is*, forget that, in their outcry in behalf of every existing book, and paragraph, and sentence, and word in the present edition of it, as 'God's Word written,' they are simply begging the question, What *is* 'God's Word written'? What *is*, without any doubt, a genuine portion of those writings which contain the message from God? The question is, in no case, 'Will you part with any utterance of God's voice, whether through apostle or evangelist?' but only, 'Is this particular word, or sentence, or passage, truly such an utterance? Have we good grounds for accepting it as such? Nay, have we not overwhelming grounds for doubting it to be such?' We do right to hold fast 'the faith once delivered to the saints,' but the more we are determined to be faithful to this faith, just the more sedulous and more searching must be our inquiry, Have we here this faith in its integrity?"

 THOMAS GRIFFITH, late Prebendary of St. Paul's, London:
      The Gospel of the Divine Life, p. 418.

IV.

The wrong use of the Bible.

"Every Scripture inspired of God is also profitable for teaching, for reproof, for correction, for instruction in righteousness; that the man of God may be perfect, thoroughly furnished unto all good works."— 2 Tim. iii; 16-17.

"USE the world as not abusing it" was a great principle of the Apostle, which has many special applications. One of these comes again before us to-day: Use the Bible as not abusing it.

I proceed to point out some further wrong uses of the Bible:

I.

It is a wrong use of the Bible to go to it as an authority in any sphere save the spheres of theology and of religion.

In the traditional view it was an infallible authority upon every subject of which it treated.

The Divine Being had prepared a book which answered off-hand the questions man's mind naturally starts concerning the problems of existence; a book which taught officially how the earth came into its present form, how life arose upon it, how man was made, how sin entered, how the world was peopled, how mankind was to fare upon the earth, how the present order was to come to an end, and many things beside. To answer authoritatively these questions was the *raison d'etre* of the Bible. It laid a solid foundation for a science of life. With the passing away of the unreal Bible all reference to it for such information should cease. These books, as actual human writings, the studies of men of long past centuries, of men having no guarantees of infallibility, cannot be expected to have anticipated the solution of the great problems of knowledge, towards which the human intellect has been laboriously working through the generations since they were written; towards whch it is still toilsomely striving, content, even now, with the cold, grey light as of the dawning day.

Our truer idea of revelation—the evolution of nature and the historic growth of man—forbids such a notion of any book. It has plainly pleased the Most High that knowledge of these mysteries should come to man through his patient, persevering effort after truth. Such continued endeavour wins gradually better knowledge, and with it better life. This process of human discovery is yet more truly a process of the Divine self-revealing. In each and every real knowledge man is learning to know—God. Each truth of science is a manifestation of somewhat in the Infinite Power in whom we live and move and have our being. Had it pleased God to have given, centuries ago, a super-natural answer to these problems of earth, He would simply have dismissed His children from school, with-held from them that noble education which lies in the discipline of study, and, while giving them truth, have robbed them of that keenest joy of life, that benediction richer even than the possession of truth—the search for it.

How indeed, even in the resources of omnipotence, could an answer to the earth-problems have been framed, which, while coming down to the plane of the age of Moses, should have kept level with the rise of human knowledge through the climbing centuries? No, the Bible was not prepared as an Encyclopedia of Knowledge for the successive generations of men. Its writers may anticipate the thought of ages by profound intuitions, pregnant imaginations, visions of the seer, as Plato does. Genius often outstrips the plodding feet of generations. But genius must not put on the airs of omniscience. It must submit its claims to trial by jury. They are to stand, if stand they shall, not because they are in Genesis or the Republic, but because they prove true.

When (*e. g.*) the Biblical writers speak of the Creation, the Garden of Eden, the Fall of Man, etc., they give us their thoughts, the thoughts of their age, the thoughts of earlier ages, of greatly gifted minds in many ages gathering into an imposing tradition; which, as we now see, came down through successive generations of Hebrews, from a remote antiquity in which this race had not been thrown off from the common Semitic stock. On the baked clay tablets of Babylonia we read to-day the same stories. The Hebrews worked them over, under the plastic power of their religious genius, into the lofty ethical and theistic forms in which they stand in Genesis; forms which, rightly read, are parables fresh and inspiring now, as when, twenty-five hundred years ago, Jewish children listened to them with awe beneath the willows by the water courses of Babylonia. That most exquisite story of our weird Hawthorne, the Marble Faun, is a version of the legend of the Garden of Eden. Commingled with these lofty truths we find crude notions of astronomy, geology, biology, and anthropology. How could it be otherwise, since these sciences were embryotic then, or even unborn? We hearken, reverently, thankfully, to the philosophy and poetry of Hebrew, Chaldean and Accadian sages and seers, in these profound and subtle parables of the mysteries which still fascinate us. We dismiss the knowledge of nature set forth in these legends and myths as the child-sciences of Israel and Chaldea and Accadia.

We go to our savans for knowledge of physical nature. We make no attempt to reconcile Genesis with the Origin of Species. Genesis is no authority in science, and The Origin of Species is no authority in philosophy, poetry, theology or religion.

The accounts of man in the dim distance of pre-historic times, given in Genesis, belong to the departments of the antiquarian, and the philologist; and we trust their story, no matter how it collides with the Hebrew traditions. So through every sphere of knowledge upon which the Biblical writers enter, outside of their own special spheres, we follow them as venerable guides, but as entirely fallible authorities, expressing the knowledge of their age and race.

Thus, to take one example from later times, St. Paul, in the first epistle to the Corinthians, condemns woman's participation in the exercises of worship and instruction in the Christian assemblies of Corinth. This judgment is accepted, by those who hold to the unreal Bible, as forclosing the case of woman versus man in the vocation of the ministry, in this land and age as in all lands and ages. We saw lately the action of this theory over in Brooklyn. Though she had the gifts and graces of a Lucretia Mott, though her preaching were blessed as that of a Miss Smiley, though woman's temperament seems peculiarly fitted for the inspirational influences of the pulpit, yet Nature's ordination must be disowned because Saul of Tarsus thought it unseemly for a woman to speak in meeting! He thought it unseemly also, as he tells us in the same letter, that woman should appear unveiled in public assemblies; in which you do not seem to consider him an authority. Why should you defer to him in the one opinion and disregard him in the other? Both opinions formed part of his education as a Jew of the first century of our era; as which he frankly confessed that he regarded woman as inferior to man. We do not consider the Jewish physiology and psychology of that age binding on us; and St. Paul's opinion on such a matter falls to the ground with it.

II.

It is a wrong use of the Bible, for the purposes of theology or religion, to give its language any other meaning than that which similar language would have under similar circumstances.

People of sound minds do not read poetic language in other books as though it were prose. They do not take words thrown off at white heat; crowd them, all molten with feeling, into the mould of a Gradgrind understanding; force them to take the form of such matter-of-fact minds; and then, when the emotion is cooled down, and the fluent fancies are reduced to stiff, hard prose, say

—"there, that is the exact meaning of this language!" Fancy Shakespeare's impetuous, tumultuous, riotous imagery treated by such 'criticism!'

Yet that is the sort of treatment which many learned pedants call 'expounding the Bible!' It is with the greatest difficulty that the Western mind can rightly read the Eastern's language. We miss the rich aroma of their nectared speech, and find only the grounds left. And we take these grounds for the true original beverage of the gods! Out of such residuum of poetry, when the poesy has exhaled, we make our spiritual food! Poetry petrified into prose—is the real explanation to be offered of many an absurdity of Bible-reading.

A visitor to one of the Shaker communities describes the men and women as engaging in the most preposterous play of making-believe; performing upon imaginary instruments as they marched in procession; going through the motions of washing their faces and hands as they surrounded an imaginary fountain; and, finally, plunging bodily into this spiritual fountain, by rolling over on the grass! To an exclamation of surprise at such childish doings, answer was made that thus they were becoming as little children, in order to enter the kingdom of heaven! *

Luther sat disputing with Zwinglius the doctrine

---

* "History of American Socialisms,"—Noyes.—p. 608.

of trans-substantiation, and to every argument of his rational opponent answered by laying his sturdy finger on the words, "This *is* my body." The most powerful Church of Christendom bases itself upon this prosaic reading of a poetic saying.

Many a mysterious dogma would simplify itself at once by remembering that, in the language of the imagination, "the letter killeth, but the spirit giveth it life." *

We are not to rush from this extreme into the opposite error and turn into mystical and marvellous meanings the plain sense of the Biblical writers. Imagine the result of putting all sorts of mystic glosses on the straight-forward accounts of men and things in ordinary writings. Such is in reality the folly of turning the sober statements of Biblical prose writers into allegories, parables, symbols, types; and of finding underneath the plainest meanings a double, triple and quadruple sense.

In the hour of Christ's approaching arrest he warns his disciples, in His usual figurative manner, that they must now learn to provide for themselves; since he would shortly be taken from them. "He that hath a purse let him take it; and he that hath no sword let him sell his garment and buy one." And

---

* "To understand that the language of the Bible is fluid, passing "and literary, not rigid, fixed and scientific, is the first step towards "a right understanding of the Bible."—*Literature and Dogma :*—p. xii.

his disciples, being very unimaginative folk, or being perhaps stupefied with wonder and anxiety by His strange words and actions on that night of sad surprises, said—" Lord, behold here are two swords." The Master answered, with a weariness of their obtuseness that we can feel in the curt reply, "It is enough." And the wisdom of the Roman Church sees herein a type of the temporal and spiritual power of the Papacy!

I am solemnly warned against such learned puerilities every time I turn to my shelves and encounter Swedenborg's "Arcana Cœlestia." In ten goodly volumes he interprets Scripture history after this fashion:

" 'And Rebecca arose'—hereby is signified an elevation of the affection of truth: 'And her damsels'—hereby are signified subservient affections: 'And they rode upon camels'—hereby is signified the intellectual principle elevated above natural scientifics."!

Of all this pious sort of folly we may say with the Master—" Enough."

It is the common mistake which gathers a nimbus of mystic sense around every book excessively revered. Thus the Greeks fancied an inner and mystical sense in Homer; and thus Italian professors expound the esoteric significance of Dante.

The fantastic dream of mysterious meanings in the Bible must take wings after its kindred fancies of

Greeks and Italians, at the touch of a ripening literary judgment. One rule holds of all human letters. Where there is legend, myth, metaphor, or other clear form of poetic fancy, language is to be read imaginatively. Otherwise, in the Bible, as out of it, the ordinary meaning of words must be followed.

III.

It is a wrong use of the Bible to construct a theology out of it, by the mechanical system of proof texts in vogue in the churches.

With a preconceived system of thought in their minds, drawn from the most highly evolved speculations of the New Testament, men have gone through both Testaments; and whenever they have lighted upon a sentence which seemed to coincide with this system, it has been torn bleeding from its place in a living texture of thought, impaled on some one of the "Five Points," and set up in the Theological Cabinet, duly labelled "Proof-Text of Original Sin," or "Proof Text of Future Punishment."

What a monstrosity an ordinary Sunday School Scripture Catechism is, with its statements of received doctrines, to which are appended proof-texts drawn from Genesis and Isaiah and Paul; *i.e.*, from some pre-historic tradition, from a Hebrew statesman's oration and from a Christian apostle's letter. It makes no difference what the character of the writing from which the sentence is taken. Everything is grist for this mill. A "judgment" or "doom" of the nomadic Hebrews, a burning metaphor from a late poet and a metaphysical proposition from an Alexandrian philosopher are jumbled together, side by side, as co-equal proofs of the most awful doctrines.

An ancient historian, gathering up the traditions of his primitive fore-fathers, records the legend of the Flood, in which it is told that

> "God saw that the wickedness of man was great in the earth,
> And that every imagination of the thoughts of his heart
> Was only evil continually."

The poet who wrote, out of the deep of some experience of shameful sin, the pathetic penitential hymn, known as the Fifty-first Psalm, said, in the course of his self-condemnings:—

> "Behold I was shapen in wickedness,
> And in sin hath my mother conceived me."

The poet who wrote his unrivaled prophecies amid the humiliation of the national exile in Babylonia, cried out in one place:—

> "We are all as an unclean thing,
> And all our righteousness are as filthy rags."

And these mythic and poetic words, true to man's abiding sense of evil in his deepest hours, stand to-day in the arsenal of theology as proof-texts of the doctrines of original sin and total depravity!

Even this folly has been surpassed. Among the proverbial sayings of the Jews was one to this effect;

"If the tree fall towards the South, or towards the North,
In the place where the tree falleth, there it shall be."

The meaning of such a proverb is surely plain enough. Death's action is irrevocable. As it meets a man it leaves him. His plans and schemes lie as incapable of development as the fallen tree is incapable of new sproutings. At the time the book of Ecclesiastes was written, the belief in any life after death was little known in Israel. This book was the work of a thorough pessimist, whose constant refrain was—Vanity of Vanities, all is Vanity. It gives no hint of a second life; and in the absence of this faith the present life is to the writer an insoluble problem. This saying really expressed the popular belief that death ended everything. A man falls like a tree, and, like a prostrate tree, as he falls he lies.

And lo! this Jewish proverb is the first proof-text generally quoted for the dread doctrine that after death there is another life, but that its character is fixed forever by the state of the man at death; the dogma of everlasting conscious suffering in Hell!

What Midsummer Night's Dream reasoning, turning common-sense topsy-turvy, and treating the words of God in the very reverse way from that in which all sane people agree to treat the words of man!

IV.

It is a wrong use of the Bible to disregard the chronological order of its parts in constructing our theology.

We are not to read the Biblical writers as though they were all cotemporaries. They are separated by vast tracts of time. The later writers stand upon the shoulders of their predecessors and see further and clearer. We are not to view the institutions or doctrines of the Bible as though, no matter in what period of the development of the Hebrew Nation or of the Christian Church they are found, they were equally authoritative upon us. That would be to say that green apples are as good food for us as ripe ones. The time-perspective is essential to set any Biblical institution or dogma in the true light.

Romanists and our own Ritualists entrench their sacerdotalism behind the priestly system of the Jews. As though, because that was once needful and serviceable to an ignorant, half heathen people, it was still indispensible to us. As though what providence once ordained, providence perpetually imposed on humanity. Such a rule would keep us with our primers always in our hands. Progress is marked by the debris of discarded institutions, wholesome and necessary once, but incumbrances after a time. The whole *rationale* of sacerdotalism is exploded by this simple common sense principle; and we see in its light the significance of Paul's impatient sweeping away of the Law; of the entire ignoring of the sacrifice and the priesthood in the life and teaching of Jesus himself.

"The hour cometh when ye shall neither in this mountain,
Nor yet at Jerusalem, worship the Father. God is spirit;
And they that worship must worship him in spirit and in truth."

Dogmas also must be seen in historical perspective. Thus, for example, the doctrine of the Second Advent, which still exercises the Christian mind, is wholly cleared up as looked at through the time-vista.

We see the progress of the Messianic expectation through the centuries immediately prior to the age of Christ, in our old Testament books and in the Apocryphal writings. In these latter works we see it gradually gathering round itself visions of the winding up of the present aeon, the renovation of the earth, the judgment of the nations, the resurrection of the pious dead, and the opening of a millenial era in which the Messiah should rule the world from Jerusalem. It would appear to have even developed the notion that the Messiah, after his appearance on earth, would depart into the spirit-world, to consummate his preparation; and would return thence to assume full power. This had became the popular expectation by the Christian era.

When then the early Christians became satisfied that Jesus was the Messiah, it followed of necessity that they should after his death, say to themselves — "He has gone into the heavens to receive his institution into the office he has won by his sinless life and suffering death. He will come again in the clouds with power; the conquering Messiah."

This belief seems to have taken shape first in Paul's fervid mind. His earlier epistles were full of it. His converts became unsettled by it, and in their excited expectation of the return of the Messiah they neglected their earthly duties; and Paul had to caution them against this impatience and cool their heated minds.

This and other experiences sobered Paul's own mind. He found that as year after year came round the Messiah did not return. In the rapid ripening of thought which went on in the tropical climate of his soul, he grew into a more spiritual apprehension of Christ. If you read his undoubted letters in the order of their writing; First Thessalonians,

First and Second Corinthians, Galatians, Romans, etc., you will note a steady decrease of reference to this topic, until it fades away into a vague vision of the dawning day of God; the absolute assurance that Christ would conquer and rule the earth, though it might be in the spirit and not in the flesh; the certain conviction of a good time coming though beyond his ken. The later light of the apostle corrected his earlier misapprehensions; and would correct our crude and carnal notions of the second coming of Christ, if we would only study Paul, as we study Turner or Shakespeare, in his ripening 'periods.'

Were this one principle followed, our popular theology would soon reconstruct itself.

V.

It is a wrong use of the Bible to cite its authors as of equal authority, even in the spheres of theology and religion.

The teachings of any human writing come clothed with such authority as the author's name lends to it or its intrinsic force wins for it.

If in the work of an obscure economic writer, of no perceptible ability, you come upon the theory that the land of a people belongs to the people; that its passing into the absolute ownership of private persons is the basic evil of our civilization; that the nation must resume the inalienable rights of the people at large, in the resources of all wealth, and regulate the individual usufruct of land in the interests of the entire body politic—you will probably toss the book contemptuously from you as the crazy lucubration of a fool.

If in reading John Stuart Mill's Principles of Political Economy you come upon this theory, cautiously broached, you are constrained to treat it with the consideration due an acknowledged master in this science. If again in the first elaborate work of a new author, Progress and Poverty, you meet this same theory, boldly laid down as the central theme of the book, and contended for as the real solution of the persistent problem of pauperism, you are disposed to pass it by unheeded. The author's name carries to your mind no prestige of tradition. He speaks from no time-honored university chair. No array of imposing titles hang upon the plain 'Henry George,' of the title page. But you become interested in these brilliant pages of genius and follow the author, with growing sympathy, to the end.

You lay the book down, feeling as though a spell had been upon you, in which you could form no sound judgment. You lay it by accordingly, to take it up after some weeks, work over its positions, and find your first impressions confirmed; to realize that here is a work of real, rare power; an epoch-making book, which, if it does not carry your conviction, commands your careful consideration.

Precisely so we are to be affected by the Biblical authors. There are writings in the Bible by utterly unknown writers. A letter of an obscure author cannot come with the weight of a letter from St. Paul. There are writings of widely different mental force. Biblical authors varied in personal power as much as other authors. Inspiration cannot do away with the limitations of the human individuality. It must be modified by its instrumentality. The saints are of various orders. Even the diamond books which reflect the light of God so brilliantly may not be all of first water. We must allow for the hues in the less perfect prisms. Were the greatest musical genius in the world to sit before the key-boards he could not draw from a harmonium the notes of a Lucerne organ. The impact of a writing on our souls must be proportionate to the spiritual and ethical force with which it is charged. Everyone recognizes this practically. None of us, however orthodox, professes to be as much inspired by Esther as by Job; by Chronicles as by Kings; by Daniel as by Isaiah; by Jude as by Paul. That simply means that there is not as much inspiration in some Biblical authors as in others.

No author is always at his best. His work differs. The second epistle to the Thessalonians is not level with the epistle to the Romans. The third epistle of John, if it be of John, is surely not as highly inspired as the first epistle of John. Inspiration is plainly a matter of degrees.

The recognition of this common-sense principle, theoretically, would remand the darker doctrines of Christianity to such authority as the lower order of Biblical writings possess. The terrifying and torturing teachings of the New Testament are from obscure authors, or from the masters in their lower moods. The representations of a wrathful God, of an avenging Christ, of a hell of horrors, are found in such epistles as Second Thessalonians, whose authorship is uncertain; as Jude or Second Peter, about whose authorship and date we have only the probability that no apostle wrote them, and that they were written after the first, fresh inspiration had passed from the church. Rabbinical speculations and Greek superstitions show themselves at work in the Christian Church.* The unquestioned letters of Paul are sunny and sweet. In them we see the father of Christian Restorationism. If he knows anything of a dark side to the resurrection, as he shows elsewhere

---

* The revised version calls the attention of English readers to this latter influence, in the marginal rendering of "*Tartarus*" for "Hell" in 2 Peter, ii: 4.

that he does, he leaves it in its own shadows; and in the height of this great argument of Corinthians brings to the front only the resurrection to life and joy. "Knowing the fear of the Lord we —— persuade men."

The first epistle of John is true to its favorite symbol of the light. There are no clouds in it. The God revealed in the greatest writings of the greatest authors of the New Testament is Love. The Christ they picture is *Christus Consolator*. The full breath of inspiration opens only the upper register of notes. The voices of the soul are buoyant, joyous, hopeful.

If you are willing to follow the most inspired writers, in their most inspired moods, up into the heights whither the divine afflatus bore them, you will mount above the cloud-level, and leave to those who lag after feebler guides on the lower ranges of truth, the chill mists that eat into the soul, while you rejoice in the light.

VI.

It is a wrong use of the Bible to manufacture out of it any one uniform system of theology, as the fixed and final form of thought in which religion is to live.

Let me define these contrasting terms, so commonly confounded. Religion is man's perception of the Power in whom we live and move and have our being, and his emotion towards this power. Theology is man's conception of this Power, and his thought defined and formulated.

Religion is man's feeling after God; theology is man's grasp of God. The two are necessarily connected. They are different forms of one and the same force; the heat and the light which stream from God; but the heat and the light are not always equal. A worthy thought of God ought to sustain any worthy feeling towards Him. It generally does so. A heightened thought of God may often be found back of a rising flow of feeling after Him. More often the emotion precedes the conception; the vague, awed sense of God travails till a new thought is born among men. This has been the order of development in history. Men felt the Divine Power and Presence ages before they had learned so much of theology as to say—God. The feeling of God—religion—always keeps, in healthy natures, far ahead of theology—the thought about Him. The deepest religion finds no word for the mystery before which it bows. Its only thought may be that no thought is sufficient.

"In that high hour thought was not."

Theology, then, as man's thought about God, is

necessarily conditioned by man's mind. It is under the general limitations of the human intellect, and the special limitations of thought in each race and age and individuality. It cannot escape these limitations, expand as they may. A flooding of the mind from on high may overflow these embankments, but they still stand, shaping the flow of the fullest tides. The individuality of a great writer asserts itself most strongly in his greatest works. His deepest inspiration brings out most plainly his mental form, just as the drawing of a full breath shows the real shape of a man. No possible theory of inspiration should lead us to look for the submergences of the dykes of thought cast up by race and age and individuality.

As a matter of fact, we find no uniformity in the theologies of the New Testament writers. Men have tried hard to make it appear that there was such a unity of thought. Never was more ingenious joiner-work done than in the "harmonies" of the New Testament writers. But facts are stubborn things, and in this case have resisted even the omnipotence of human ingenuity; as open minds have seen, despite the doctors.

St. Paul's Epistles reveal a theology by no means as precise and fixed as is popularly imagined, undergoing rapid changes, growing with his growth, always suffused from the soul with emotions which struggled against the prison bars of thought and speech. His intensely speculative mind had furnished a system of thought into which he built such ideas as these: The pre-existence of Christ, as, in some mystic, undefined way, the Head of Humanity; the sacrificial nature of His death; the justification of the sinner through faith; the life of Christ within the soul, as the Human Ideal; the speedy return of Christ in person to reign on earth (at least in the early part of his career); the resurrection of the pious dead; the translation of living believers; the final victory of goodness over evil; and the ending of the mediatorship of Christ, God then becoming all in all.

This was the form which the mystery of God's relationship to man took in the mind of this great genius, and around which the fiery passion of his hunger after righteousness shaped itself.

In the Epistle of St. James, assuming the traditional authorship, how much of this theology can you find? The incarnation is nowhere clearly stated. The name of Christ occurs but twice. His atonement is scarcely mentioned. The prophets are held up as examples of patience, under suffering, without any reference to Christ. Paul's especial doctrine of justification by faith is explicitly denied. Of his fellowship with the Gentiles and his broad human sympathies, there is nothing whatever. All is intensely Jewish. If Paul's theology is orthodoxy, James is dreadfully unsound.* "The fundamentals" are all lacking Both Paul and James differ very decidedly from the mystic soul who wrote the First Epistle of John; and all three differ again, quite as much, from the philosopher who wrote the Epistle to the Hebrews. How little have either the Apocalypse or Jude in common with Paul! We can no more make a uniform theology out of the New Testament writers than we can out of Calvinism, Arminianism, Catholicism, and Unitarianism.

These various theologies can be traced to the elements making up the individualities of the different writers. The idiosyncracies of Paul are clearly marked. He was a man of strong speculative mind, of mystic piety, of lofty enthusiasm for great ideals, a-hungered after righteousness. A Jew and yet a Roman citizen, his education developed the two-fold sympathies of an Israelite of the dispersion. At the feet of the liberal rabbi, Gamaliel, he learned the curious and mystical lore of the rabbins, while drinking in from his Master the spirit of freedom. Thrown from a child in constant contact with the Gentiles of his native city, Tarsus, race prejudices had been sapped unconsciously; while in youth or manhood the wisdom

---

*Luther's strong sense detected his unevangelicalness.

and beauty of the Greek genius had apparently been opened to him.

Paul's personality, fusing the materials of his education, and out of them building a body of thought around The Christ, explains his theology. He reproduces the conceptions of the rabbis, of the popular Jewish belief, of Gamaliel, of Tarsus, of Athens; transfigured on the heights of thought to which he climbed, in his intense musings over the problem of Jesus of Nazareth, while buried away in Arabia.

The small amount of theology in the practical Epistle of James is quite as plainly Jewish, of the school of the Sages, with a touch of Essenism. The theology of the Epistle to the Hebrews shows throughout the influences of the philosophy of Alexandria. The theology of the introduction to the Gospel according to St. John is just as unquestionably this same Alexandrian philosophy, still further developed.

These variant schools of Christian theology, so plainly revealing the sources of their variations, deny the existence of any one uniform system of thought in the New Testament writers, and pronounce the different systems transient and not final forms.

Whatever the Church may offer us, the New Testament offers us no fixed and final body of thought.

In the Bible, Christian theology is still a soft vase, plastic to the touch of each worker upon it. Had Paul's fine hand played around it even another decade, how different the shape it might have taken.

With the incoming of a more rational, ethical, and spiritual age, we may surely expect a finer fashioning of the forms of thought blocked out in the New Testament, under the first, fresh inspiration of the age of Jesus; into whose larger patterns shall be taken up all the truths revealed through the various sciences of these rich later ages; while all shall still take on the shape of Him who is the image of the invisible God.

"The Lord has more truth yet to break forth out of His holy word."

The true Biblical theology is—Christ himself. His thought of God, and not even Paul's thoughts about Christ, are to mould our thinking. The Supreme Son of Man must have had the truest thought of God. Two words formulate his theology, as bodied not in a creed, but in a prayer— "Our Father." The earliest, simplest, deepest cry of the human after God, now by Him who lived its spirit perfectly, the trusting, loving, holy Child of the Father, made no longer a sigh, a dream, a vision, but a life. "The life was the light of men."

That light is the sufficient clue to the dark labyrinth in which we wander wearily.

I cannot always make out the face of a Father on the stern, harsh Power in whom we live and move and have our being. Then I turn to my Divine Brother, who, of all the children of men, saw deepest into the mystery, and in his far-mirroring eyes I read the vision which satisfies me.

With poor dying Joe, I whisper to myself:

"'Our Father:' yes, that's werry good."

V.

The Right Critical Use of the Bible.

"I am convinced that the Bible becomes even more beautiful the more one understands it; that is, the more one gets insight to see that every word, which we take generally and make special application of to our own wants, has had, in connection with certain circumstances, with certain relations of time and place, a particular, directly individual reference of its own."

GOETHE: quoted by M. Arnold in "The Great Prophecy of Israel's Restoration."

V.

The Right Critical use of the Bible.

"God, who at many times and in many manners spake in time past to the fathers, by the prophets."—Hebrews, i. 1.

THE right use of the Bible grows out of the true view of the Bible.

The Old Testament is the literature of the people of religion, in whom ethical and spiritual religion grew, through all moods and tenses, toward perfection. The New Testament is the literature of the movement which grew out of Israel, the literature of the Universal Church bodying around the Son of Man, in whom religion came to perfect flower and fruit. The real Bible is the record of this real revelation coming through real ethical and spiritual inspirations; a revelation advancing with men's deepening inspirations toward the Light which rose in the Life of Jesus Christ our Lord.

God, who at many times and in many manners spake in time past to the fathers by the prophets, hath at the last of these days spoken unto us by a Son.

These speakings of the Divine Spirit in the souls of men, at many times and in many manners, were articulated, as best was possible, in the writings of many ages and of many forms. The Bible is the collection of these writings. They require a critical study, as *bona fide* "letters," before we can know the degree of their inspiration, and their place in the progressive historic revelation; before we can thus deduce aright the thoughts about God out of which we are to construct our theology. Concerning this right critical use of the Bible, I propose now to offer some practical suggestions. Next Sunday I purpose giving you a bird's-eye view of the general course of the historic revelation which led up to the Christ, the Word of God. After which I shall pass on to consider with you the pre-eminently right use of the Bible, in which our souls humbly hearken for its words proceeding from out the mouth of God, on which man liveth; and on them feeding, grow toward a perfect manhood in Christ Jesus.

I.

Every aid of outward form should be used to make these books appear as living "letters" to us.

The traditional form in which the Bible has been given to the people would seem to have been devised with a design of robbing its writings of every natural charm, as the best means of making men feel its supernatural power. The fresh sense of "letters" disappears in this conventional form. These many books of many ages have been bound up together, with the most imperfect classification either as to period or character. A verse-making machine has been driven through them all alike, chopping them up into short, arbitrary, artificial sentences, formally numbered in the body of the text. The larger divisions into chapters have been made in an equally mechanical manner. By this twofold system an admirable provision has been made for checking the flow of the writer's thought, and for effectually preventing any easy grasp of the natural movement of the book. Poetry has been printed as prose; thereby marring its rhythm, concealing its structure, and blinding the reader to the dramatic character of immortal works of genius. Through the whole mass of writings a system of chapter-headings has been introduced that ingeniously insinuates into the body of these sacred books, as seemingly an integral part thereof, a scheme of interpretation which possesses now no pepsine power for resolving their contents into spiritual nutriment, but rather positively hinders our assimilation of many of these books.

Probably the greatest obstacle to the use of the Bible is the senseless form in which custom persists in publishing it. I know few stronger evidences of the intrinsic power of these books than their continued influence, under conditions that would have remanded other books to the topmost shelves of the most unused alcoves in our libraries.

We ought to have the different books, or groups of books, bound separately; arranged paragraphically like other writings, with the present verse divisions indicated, if need be, in the margin; and the poetic structure properly indicated. These books should have brief, simple, lucid notes; drawing from our best critics the needful information as to their age, authorship, integrity, form, scope, obsolete words and idioms, local customs, historical allusions, etc.; with other readings throwing light upon obscure passages. Each book should be thus provided with such a popular critical apparatus as accompanies good editions of other classics, and as Matthew Arnold has prepared for one book, in his primer entitled "The Great Prophecy of Israel's Restoration;" which is the second section of Isaiah, arranged as a "Bible-reading for schools."

This series of Bible-books should then be chronologically arranged, as far as the conclusions of the higher criticism will allow; and should be bound in uniform style and set in a Bible case, preserving thus the unity of the whole. Such an edition of the Bible would stimulate a renewed resort to it, in which men would re-discover a lost literature.

Until you can procure such an edition, provide yourselves with a paragraph Bible, following the natural divisions of the writings and maintaining their poetic form; and seek the information you may desire in some of the manuals embodying the results of the higher criticism.

II.

Each writing having an intrinsic unity should, by such aids, be studied as a whole.

Every intelligent Christian ought to have a clear conception of the general scope of thought in each great Bible-book. Whatever fragmentary use of these books for direct devotional purposes may be made, he who would count himself as one of "the men of the Bible," ought to know as much about them as he knows about his favorite authors.

Who that pretends to be a lover of Shakespeare is content with a scrappy reading of his immortal plays? To enjoy them fully, even in fragmentary readings, he seeks to have a foundation of critical knowledge, such as Shakespearian scholars place within the easy mastery of any one. After such a study of a play he can pick it up in leisure hours and see new beauties every time he reads it. How many Bible Christians know their Bible thus?

What a revelation such a study makes! It is an alchemist's touch, turning many a leaden book into finest gold.

The oldest book, as a whole, in the Bible, is the Song of Songs. Attributed by later ages to Solomon, it was probably written by some unknown author, anywhere from the tenth to the eighth century before Christ.* The poem is dramatic in form, though imperfectly constructed according to our canons. Its scenes shift, and its speakers change with true dramatic movement. It is the closest approach to the drama preserved to us in Hebrew literature, whose genius never favored this highly organic form. There is needed but the usual indication of the *dramatis personæ* to clear the movement of the plot, and to reveal the force and beauty of the poem.

A maiden, her royal admirer, ladies of the court, the girl's brother and her shepherd lover, appear and disappear in animated conversation. The country maiden is wooed away from her shepherd lad by the allurements of a royal admirer, who employs all the resources of fervid flattery and passionate persuasion to win her as a new attraction for his harem. He is foiled, however, by her simple, steadfast loyalty to her absent lover, to whom she at length returns, triumphant in her virtue. In a corrected version, the sensuousness of our English translation disappears in the ordinary richness of Eastern imagery, and the poem becomes a pure picture of loyal love. It reveals thus the healthy moral tone of Jewish society in that early age. This sound domestic virtue of the people, which looked with abhorrence on the licentiousness of the court, becomes all the more

---

* Ewald says the tenth century, and Kuenen the eighth century.

striking in contrast with the polygamous customs of the surrounding nations. We see the social foundation on which Israel builded such a noble structure of ethical religion. The people whose literature opens with such a laud of loyal love might well rise into the pure splendors of a Second Isaiah.

Such a poem fitly introduces the canon of Scripture; since, into whatever heights Religion aspires to lift the fabric of civilization, she must lay its corner-stone in the marriage bond, and rear the church and the state upon the family.

Perhaps we may also find in this Hebrew Song of Songs that mystic meaning, not uncommon in Eastern love-songs, at least in later readings of them, which Edwin Arnold has so vividly brought out in the Hindoo Song of Songs; and may understand how the Church came to take it as a parable of the love of the soul for its Heavenly Ideal, seen in the Christ.

Job, thus read, becomes a semi-dramatic poem, in which the problem of the disconnection of goodness and good-fortune, the lack of any just ordering of individual life, is discussed in the persons of an upright and sorely afflicted patriarch and his three friends, who come to condole and counsel with him. Through their interchanging colloquies, that bring up one after another the stock theories of the age of the author, the argument moves along without really getting on. No solution is found for the perplexing puzzle, in which man's moral instincts beat vainly against the hard facts of life. Once, for a moment, the thought of a future life flashes up, as the true solution of the injustice of earth, in that thrilling cry of the tortured soul:

> I know that my Redeemer liveth,
> And that he shall stand at the latter day upon the earth:
> And though, after my skin, worms destroy this body,
> Yet out of my flesh shall I see God;
> Whom I shall see for myself,
> And mine eyes shall behold, and not as a stranger.

But the vision fades upon an atmosphere unready for it, and the poet does not return to follow this clue out into the sunshine.

All the light that he can discern is in Nature's manifestations of power and order and wisdom. From a wide range of knowledge, the poet draws together upon the stage the wonders of creation, which, with daring freedom, he introduces God himself as describing; until at length Job humbles himself in an awe not uncheered by trust:

> Therefore have I uttered that I understood not.
> Things too wonderful for me which I knew not.
> . . . .
> I have heard of Thee by the hearing of the ear;
> But now mine eye seeth Thee.
> Wherefore I abhor myself,
> And repent in dust and ashes.

By dropping out the episode of Elihu, as an insertion of some later hand, the movement of the poem becomes sustained and progressive. The arguments of the Jewish theology are cleverly presented, while the swift, sure sense of justice in the sufferer pierces all sophisms, and riddles all pious conventionalities. The descriptions of Nature are graphic and eloquent. The *motif* of the drama is one that voices the thought and feeling of our far-off age, in which many men again vainly thresh the old arguments of conventional theology, in trying to solve the "godless look of earth," and take refuge anew in the manifestations of power and law in nature; not without the ancient lesson, let us trust, of an awe which silences and purifies, and leaves them in the light as of a mystery of meaning on the sphynx's face, breaking into the dawning of a day which "uttereth speech." Scientific agnosticism, in so far as it is an humble confession of human ignorance, has its worship scored in this noble poem, ringing the changes on the strain, at once plaint and praise:

> Canst thou by searching find out God?
> Canst thou find out the Almighty unto perfection?
> It is as high as heaven; what canst thou do?
> Deeper than hell; what canst thou know?

Curiously enough, as showing the power of conventionalism, the author winds up with a prose epilogue of the genuine story-book fashion, in which all things are set right by Job's restoration to his lost wealth, in multiplied possessions. Pathetic persuasion of the poor human heart that all things must come right in the end!

What the Epistle to the Romans, that affrighting *vade mecum* of theological disputants, becomes when read thus reasonably as a whole, with critical discernment of its real aim, I will not try to tell you; but will content myself with sending you where you may see it beautifully told, with Paul's own upspringing inspiration of righteousness, in Matthew Arnold's "St. Paul and Protestantism."

III.

Each great book should, as a whole, be read in its proper place in Hebrew and Christian history.

The historical method is the true clue to the interpretation of a book. To know it aright we must know the age in which it was produced. This is the method by which such surprising light has been shed on many great works. Who that has read Taine's graphic portraiture of the Elizabethan age can fail ever thereafter to see Shakespeare stand forth vividly? What can we make of Dante without some knowledge of Italy in the thirteenth century? What new life is given to Milton's Samson after we have seen the blind old poet of the fallen Protectorate in his dreary home! How can we rightly estimate Rousseau's writings unless we know somewhat of the artificial and luxurious age to which they came as a call back to nature? Taken out of their true surroundings these writings lose their force and meaning.

In the same way we need to find the historical place of a Biblical writing, and to read it in the light of its relation to the period.

The traditional view of Deuteronomy made it the last of the writings of Moses, a Farewell Address of the Father of his Country; reciting to the nation he had founded the story of its deliverance, repeating the laws established for its welfare, and warning it against the dangers awaiting it in the future. Such a view was attended with many difficulties, not insuperable, however, to the critical knowledge of earlier generations. Its real place in the history of Israel appears to have been found of late.

The Prophetic Reformation of Religion, begun in the eighth century before Christ, by the group of noble men of whom Isaiah was the most conspicuous, had, by the latter part of the seventh century before Christ, become ripe for an organization of the institutions of religion. Jeremiah was the central figure in this second period of the prophetic movement. Upon the throne of Judah at that time was the good young king, Josiah—the Edward the Sixth of Israel—in whom the hopes of the reformers centred. About the year 625 B.C. occurred an event that decided the future of religion in Judah; described in the twenty-second chapter of the second book of Kings. The high-priest sent to the young king, saying:

I have found the book of the law in the house of the Lord.

This book of the law of Moses, according to tradition, had been lost; had been lost so long that its provisions had dropped into disuse, into oblivion; an oblivion so complete that the nation's religion ignored and violated the whole system of that law; had been lost so long and so thoroughly that the very existence of such a law had passed from the memory of man.

This was the book that Hilkiah claimed to have re-discovered in the temple archives. It was at once read to the excited king. It made a profound impression upon him by its revelation of the apostasy in which the nation was living, and by its solemn threatenings upon such apostasy. .

It came to pass that when the king had heard the words of the book of the law, that he rent his clothes.

For, said he:

Great is the wrath of the Lord that is kindled against us, because our fathers have not hearkened unto the words of this book, to do according unto all that which is written concerning us.

The devout young king threw himself into a thorough reformation of the prevailing religion. All local altars were swept away, all idolatries were cleared from the Jerusalem temple, the priesthood was centred in the capital and more thoroughly organized; in short, as our fathers read the story, Mosaism was re-established, after some seven centuries of partial or total disuse.

Through processes which we cannot now follow, our later critics have, I think, fairly established the proposition, that this book of The Law was none other than the substance of our book of Deuteronomy, then for the first time written. The plans of the prophetic reformers had contemplated the sweeping changes described above, in the interests of an ethical and spiritual religion. They felt that they were but carrying out the principles of the nation's great Founder. Of his original conception of religion, bodied in The Ten Words, their aspirations were the legitimate historical development; as the leaf and bud are the growth of the far back roots. This programme of the prophetic reformers, presented in its true light as a development of the ideas of Moses, was, by the priest Hilkiah, sent to the king as the law of the nation's Founder, with the results sketched above.

Read in this light, the book takes on a fresh and fascinating interest. It marks the organization of the movement toward a higher religion which had been started by the great prophets of the preceding century. It becomes the Augsburg Confession of the Jewish Reformation, from which dates the gradual possession of the institutions of the nation by ethical and spiritual religion.

The lofty character of this book, the "St. John of the Old Testament," as Ewald called it, is thus rendered intelligible; as it stands for the aspirations of the noblest movement in ancient Jewish history. It is the issue of a long travail of soul to whose words we hearken in such a truth as this:

Hear, O Israel: The Lord our God is one Lord: and thou shalt love the Lord thy God with all thine heart, and with all thy soul, and with all thy might.

Placed in this position, the book of Deuteronomy becomes the key to Israel's history, by which criticism is reconstructing that story, on the lines of the great laws of all life, with most significant consequences to the cause of religion. The ideas and institutions known to us as The Mosaic Law come forth now as the crown and culmination of a long historic development. Israel's story is that of a slow and gradual education under the divine hand; not a relapse, but a progress, not an apostasy, but an evolution. Israel takes its place in the general order of humanity's movement. With it religion sweeps at once into the pathway of progress which science has shown to be the order of nature; and the historic revelation is seen to be, like the revelation in nature, a gradual, progressive manifestation of Him "whose goings forth are as the morning"—its orbit the sweep of the ascending sun.

With such mighty secrets does this little book

grow luminous when placed in the light of its real belongings.

The Book of Ezekiel, whose historic position was never disputed, becomes of new value in the light of a fuller knowledge of its period. It presents to the science of Biblical criticism the missing link in its theory of Israel's development. It shows the process of transformation, out of which issued during the exile the elaborate, hierarchical system known to us as Mosaism. The new criticism seems to me to have reasonably established the theorem, that the priestly cultus embodied in the legislation of the Pentateuch was first systematized into the form it there presents during the exile, and was first set up as the national system on the return to Judea. It is not claimed that it was a new manufacture of that period. As such it would be inconceivable.* It is simply claimed that it was a thorough codification, for the first time, of the scattered and conflicting codes of conduct and systems of worship of the various local priesthoods of Israel, as handed down by tradition and in records from ancient times; a codification animated by the centralizing and hierarchical tendencies working in the nation; which tendencies were themselves the result largely of the prophetic spirit, and

---

* Ask at Abel and at Dan whether the genuine old statutes of Israel have lost their force?—2 Samuel, xx. 18. Restored by Ewald from the LXX.

its aspirations for a nobler religion.* It is not difficult to account for this remarkable priestly movement.

The institutional organization of religion that began under Josiah had continued, with various fortunes, the aim of the higher spirits of the nation, down to the exile. The movement of life was in the direction of uniformity and order. There was much in the circumstances of the exile to stimulate this movement. The priests were left without their temple worship, and, in the absence of outward interests, must have turned their thought in upon their system itself, studying it as they had not done in the midst of its actual operation. Like all wrongly lost possessions, it became doubly dear. The Jews were placed in the midst of an ancient and highly organized priestly system in Babylonia, whose benefits to culture and religion they must have noted and pondered. In the national humiliation and the personal sorrows of such a wholesale carrying away of a people from their native land, a wide-spread awakening of the inner life was experienced, a genuine revival of religion. A new wave of prophetic enthusiasm rose in the strange land, lifting the soul of the nation to heights of spiritual and ethical religion never reached before.

This revival was stamped with the impress of

---

* Such a late codification is no more inconceivable than Justinian's codification of Roman law.

the intellectual influences which were working upon the Jews in Babylonia. Some of the extant writings of this period, alike in literary style, in moral tone and in religious thought, mark a new era. Israel's genius flowered in this dark night—true to the mystic character of the race. This highest effort of prophetic thought and feeling appears to have quickly exhausted itself. In reality, it followed the usual order of religious movements, and turned into a priestly organization. The group of prophets around the first Isaiah prepared the way for the priestly movement that followed a century later. The group of prophets around the second Isaiah prepared the way for the priestly movement that followed close in their steps. First comes always, in religion, an epoch of inspiration, and then comes a period of organization. The organization never bodies fully the spirit of the inspiration. The ideal is not realizable in institutions. Institutional religion is always a compromise, a mediation between the lofty conceptions and impatient aspirations of the few who inspire the new life, and the low notions and contented conventionalisms of the many whom they seek to inspire. The compromise is necessarily of the nature of a reaction; but the interplay of action and re-action is the law of ethical as of chemical forces.

Israel really needed the conserving work of a great organization. The prophetic religion was far in advance of the popular level. The high thoughts and lofty ideas of the prophets needed to be wrought into a cultus, which, while not breaking abruptly with the popular religion, should imbue the conventional forms with deeper ethical and spiritual meanings; should, through them, systematically train the people in ethical habits and spiritual conceptions; and should thus gradually educate men out of these forms themselves.

In the providence of God, and under the influences of His patient Spirit, this needful system was developed in the exile: a system whose symbolism was so charged with ethical and spiritual senses that it led on to Christ; as the Epistle to the Hebrews rightly shows and as Paul distinctly declares. As the first priestly period, following the first prophetic epoch, bodied that double movement in a book—Deuteronomy; so the second priestly period, following the second prophetic epoch, bodied this double movement in a book, or group of books—the present form of the Pentateuch. The traditions and histories and legislations of the past were worked over into a connected series of writings, through which was woven the new priestly system, in a historical form. On the restoration to Judea, this institutional reorganization was set up as the law of the land, and continued thenceforward in force—the providential instrumentality for the *ad interim* work of four centuries. Such a remarkable process of development, so deepening in us a sense of the guiding hand of God, ought to show some sign of its working, in the literature of the period. However clear, from our general knowledge, the tendencies which were at work in that period, we could not feel assured of our correct interpretation of this most important epoch, in the absence of some such sign, in a writing of that date.

The Book of Ezekiel supplies the missing link. The writer was a prophet-priest, who went into the exile, and wrote in Babylonia. In the earlier part of his life-work, recorded in the earlier portion of his book, he was thoroughly prophetic, intensely ethical and spiritual, breathing the very spirit of his great master, Jeremiah. In the latter part of his career he was visited with dreams, such as are plainly indicated to us in the remarkable vision occupying the concluding section of his book. The fortieth chapter opens thus:

> In the visions of God brought he me into the land of Israel, and set me upon a very high mountain, upon which was as the frame of a city on the south.

Then follows, through eighteen chapters, a sketch of the temple system in the expected restoration. It is a thoroughly ideal sketch, a vision destined to take on much simpler and humbler proportions in its realization; a picture probably not intended for copying in actual construction, but, like all ideal work, a powerful stimulus to the aspirations it expressed.

It is a free sketch of the New Priestly System, on the easel, awaiting correction and completion at the hands of Ezra and others. It reveals to us the visions that were occupying the minds of the best men in the latter part of the exile, and the work they were essaying. Thus we are prepared for the final issue.

The Book of Daniel has been wrongly placed, traditionally, with most serious consequences to the character of the book, and, through this misconception, to Christianity. Dated from the early part of the sixth century before Christ, its story of Daniel's experiences read as literal history, and its visions appear as actual predictions of long subsequent events.

A high authority has declared—

There can be no doubt that it exercised a greater influence upon the early Christian Church than any other writing of the Old Testament.*

That influence, owing to this misconception, is chiefly to be traced in the growth of an apocalyptic literature, and in the fantastical and material expectations of the Messianic Kingdom which they encouraged. It has continued down to our own day turning heads as wise as Sir Isaac New-

---

* Brook Foss Westcott. Smith's Bible Dictionary: article on Daniel.

THE RIGHT CRITICAL USE OF THE BIBLE. 155

ton's, setting religion at conjuring with visions of monstrous beasts and juggling with mystic figures, until the name of Prophecy has become a by-word.

This book appears to take its proper place, at least in its present form, about a century and a half before Christ. That was a period of deep depression for Israel. Under Antiochus Epiphanes the nation had been sorely oppressed, its temple defiled, and its religion well nigh crushed out. Men's hearts were failing them for fear, and for looking for those things that were coming to pass upon the earth. Pious souls turned back to the ancient time of bitter humiliation, when Israel had been scattered in a strange land, and recalled the bold word of faith spoken by Jeremiah, which had stayed the spirits of their forefathers. The great prophet promised that after seventy years the nation should be restored to its native land, and should renew its prosperity gloriously. It had won back its home, but in the old homestead it had grown poorer and feebler, generation after generation. Had the ancient promise of prophecy failed? Good men could not think so. To some devout soul came the suggestion that the seventy years had meant seventy Sabbatical years, each of which consisted of seven years; that is, four hundred and ninety years. One can still feel the thrill that must have gone through him, as he saw that this computation would place the defiling of the temple—that sign of God's having forsaken his people—in the middle of the last week of years. It was then only about three years to the destined end of the weary period that Jeremiah had included in the term of Israel's humbling, after which would come Jehovah's help. Fired with this thought, he set himself to inspire his people with fresh hope and courage.

Around a traditional Daniel, famed for his wisdom and piety, and possibly upon an earlier document containing some tales of this sage and saint, he wove a story which should interpret Jeremiah's prophecy and Jehovah's purpose. With charming grace he tells the tale of Daniel's constancy and trust under the sorest trials, and of the divine deliverance that always came to him. Into his mouth he placed predictions of what had already come to pass in history, that thus his reputation as a prophet might be established. Then he caused him to present a striking series of symbolical visions, the clue to which was furnished for the writer's contemporaries by certain clear allusions. These visions foretold deliverance as about to come at the approaching end of the four hundred and ninety years of Jeremiah. Other visions sketched the ushering in of the Messiah-Kingdom, in glowing pictures of lofty religious tone.

In that dark night over Israel this book was as the morning star. It was truly, as Dean Stanley called it, "the Gospel of the age." Its story spread, and with it spread renewed patience and hope. It doubtless fed the forces of that glorious revolt that shortly thereafter burst forth under the heroic Maccabees. Thus it kept alive the vital spark in the nation, through a crucial hour, that else might have gone out before it had given birth to Christianity. Noble as the book of Daniel is in many ways, especially as the real father of "the philosophy of history," it has a still deeper interest to us Christians for its timely service to the sinking nation through which came at last our Blessed Master.

The Acts of the Apostles, when studied in the light of the tendencies known to have been working in the apostolic church, becomes of similar importance in New Testament history to Deuteronomy in Old Testament history.

The primitive Church was, as we well know, agitated by contending factions. Two leading parties dominated all minor schools of thought; the Jewish Christians, who naturally wanted to keep within the old religion, and who would have made a reformed Judaism, and the Gentile Christians, who as naturally objected to being herded within Judaism, and who wanted to make a new and universal society. The first party rallied under the name of Peter, and the second used the name of Paul. There was imminent danger that the new society would break apart, with fatal consequences to posterity. Real and deep as were the differences between Peter and Paul, they did not, in all probability, sunder these great natures as widely as their followers imagined. There must have been meeting points between such souls, in love with the one Master. To find these convergences, and construct out of them a peace-platform on which both wings of the new society might stand, was the aim of The Acts. It embodied genuine journals of a traveling companion of St. Paul, notes of his addresses in various cities, traditions, lost to us outside of this book, of Peter's conciliatory attitude and utterances; and groups these historic fragments into a sketch, in which the two apostles are shown as dividing equally the labors of founding the Christian Church, as preaching the same views, and acting in cordial harmony.

This book is a sign of the disposition to draw together which was gaining ground among the primitive churches, a disposition fostered largely by this writing; out of which process of comprehension and conciliation arose the Catholic Church, naming its great cathedrals after St. Peter and St. Paul.

IV.

The books which are of a composite character should be read in their several parts, and traced to their proper places in history.

Thus, for example, in reading Isaiah uncritically we pass from the fragment of history that forms our thirty-ninth chapter, to the magnificent strain of impassioned imagination which opens with the fortieth chapter, as though there were no hiatus; and we proceed straight through this latter section of the book, taking it all as written in the reign of Hezekiah, that is, in the latter part of the eighth century before Christ. We thus view this second section of Isaiah from a wrong standpoint. The panorama of its visions becomes blurred. We cannot focus the glass upon the objects in its field. The real significance and beauty of this noblest reach of prophetic imagination evanishes from our vision.

To see this second section of Isaiah aright, we must push it down the stream of time nearly two hundred years. It is the work of a prophet, or group of prophets, in the latter part of the exile, about the middle of the sixth century before Christ. Watching the signs of the times, the gifted and gracious spirit who led this chorus of hope saw tokens, as of the dawning of day after the long, dark night. Rumors of the all conquering Cyrus, the Medo-Persian king, made Babylon tremble with fear, and Israel thrill with excited expectation. In the ethical and spiritual religion of the advancing Persians, the Jews might look for a bond of sympathy. It would be the policy of Cyrus to make friends of the foes of Babylon, and to place the captive people in their own land on the borders of his empire, as his grateful feudatories. The seer saw thus, in the conquering hero, the Servant of God, raised up to restore the chosen people to their native country. Prophecy kindled anew for its final flame, and burst forth in the immortal strain of hope for the long-tried Israel:

> Comfort ye, comfort ye my people,
> Saith your God.
> Speak ye comfortably to Jerusalem, and cry unto her,
> That her warfare is accomplished,
> That her iniquity is pardoned.

I never read this sublime chapter without a fresh thrill, as I hear the voice of a crushed race, lifting amid its misery a cry of unconquerable confidence in the Just and Holy One, who was ordering alike the embattled armies of earth and the starry hosts of the skies, and through history, as in nature, was sweeping on resistlessly to fulfill the good pleasure of His Will. No wonder the matchless oratorio of the Messiah opens with this aria, abruptly as the original words are spoken in Isaiah. They sound the key-note of the good tidings of great joy which, growing as a hope in men's souls through the centuries, became a faith, an assured conviction, in the life of the Christus Consolator; in whom God is seen as "Our Father which art in heaven."

Every gem of this second section of Isaiah takes on a new lustre in this setting. It is the cry of the lost sheep in the wilderness, catching sight of the Shepherd who they thought had forgotten them, that we hear in the gracious strain:

> He shall feed his flock like a Shepherd,
> He shall gather the lambs with his arm,
> And carry them in his bosom,
> And shall gently lead those that are with young.

The vision of the Suffering, Righteous Servant of God grows clear and pathetic in the true historic light. The chastened nation feels itself called to a higher mission than that of political power. It is to teach the other nations of the earth the knowledge of God. That knowledge it is itself to learn in the school of sorrow. It is to save humanity through the sacrifice of itself. Thus the secret of suffering is spelled out, not for ancient Israel alone, but for all mankind; the secret which is shrined, for ever sacred to us, in the story of our Lord Christ; from whom you and I this day, through a simple symbol, are to learn anew that if we sorrow it is that we may be made perfect through suffering, and thus be fitted to lead our fellows up into the light and love of God.

v.

These writings should be read critically, until we can decipher the successive hands working upon them, and interpret them accordingly.

Few, if any, of the books of the Bible stand now as they came from their original authors. Nearly all have been re-edited; most of them many times. Some of them have been worked over by so many hands, and have undergone such numerous and serious changes, that the original writer would scarcely identify his work. The historical writings of the Old Testament take up into them all sorts of materials, from all sorts of sources. If the annals of the Venerable Bede, the father of English history, had been re-written again and again through the subsequent centuries; abridged, enlarged, interpreted by each editor; the accumulating knowledge and growing experience of the nation read into his simple chronicles; we should appreciate the critical care needful in studying our edition of Bede if we would know the real original. Very much such care is necessary if we are to use the Old Testament histories aright for information. It is as though there were several surfaces to the parchment on which the histories were written, on each successive film of which, in finest tracery, an older record was inscribed.

Genesis, for example, presents us, at every step of what seems a consecutive story, with successive layers of tradition, through which we must work our way most carefully if we would really understand the book. We readily observe a twofold tradition of the Creation in the opening chapters of Genesis, differing very materially: a sign to us, if we need it, that there was no one authoritative account of the Creation current in Israel. Little attention is required to note a double version of the story of the flood, whose artless piecing together is the cause of the confusions and contradictions that puzzle many readers. The deciphering of this double tradition of the flood first started criticism upon the true track of Biblical study. The frequently recurring phrase, "These are the generations," or beginnings, indicates the insertion of fragments of a work giving an account of the origin of the world, of the races of earth, of language, of the Jewish people, etc.; a work called by the critics "The Book of Origins." In the fourteenth chapter there is what seems to be a very ancient non-Jewish fragment of history, torn possibly from some Syrian writing, which gives a tale of Abraham's prowess in war.

And even in one and the same tale of tradition, we apparently find strata of thought laid down by successive ages. There are extant to-day parchments in which, for lack of other material, a writer has scratched partially away an earlier manuscript, and written over it another book. Such a palimpsest is Genesis. "A legend of civilization is written over a solar-myth, and a tribal legend over the legend of civilization, and a theocratic legend over the tribal." *

When such a mastery of the Bible-books is won,

---

* "The Bible of To-day," Chadwick, p. 50.

they are to be used in the customary methods of critical study, with reference to their contents and the significances thereof, under the same general laws of interpretation that hold over other literature.

I think I hear some one saying—Is this the right use of the Bible, for which I am asked to give up the dear, old, simple way of reading for my soul's inspiration? Not at all, my friend. That blessed use of the Bible, learned at your mother's knees, is still, and must always remain, the best use possible to any one. Of this I shall speak hereafter. I am now speaking, not of the right devotional use of the Bible, but of the right critical use of it. It has been used critically in building our theologies, but, to a large extent, amiss. Out of this wrong use of it has come the misconceptions in theology which to-day perplex our minds and bar the progress of religion. If we must use the Bible critically, let us by all means try to employ a true and thorough criticism. Let us not think to close every controversy by the phrase—The Bible says so. We shall be more modest and less disputatious when we appreciate the study necessary before any one can properly answer the question—What saith the Scriptures?

Again I hear a voice from the pews—Who then save a scholar is competent for such a use of the Bible? I answer—No one, except a pupil of

THE RIGHT CRITICAL USE OF THE BIBLE. 165

the scholars. The scholars have placed within our reach the results of such a critical study of the Bible. You can find the rational guidance you may desire in the manuals which set forth the conclusions of these critical processes; though you must painfully feel, as I do, the lack of the religious tone in some of them. A crying need of our day is a Hand Book to the Bible in which the new critical knowledge shall blend, as it may blend, with the old spiritual reverence.

One should not rise from such a study of the Bible as we have made to-day, in its merely literary aspects, without a new, strange sense of awe before this mystic Book. It is the handiwork of no one man, of no group of men, of no period. It is an organic product, the growth of a whole people, the coralline structure builded by a nation. Hands innumerable have toiled over these pages. Voices indistinguishable now, in blended chorus from the dawn of history, have joined in the cry of the human after God which whispers upon us from this sacred phonograph.

Successive generations of men, struggling with sin, striving for purity, searching after God, have exhaled their spirits into the essence of religion, which is treasured in this costly vase. The moral forces of centuries, devoted to righteousness, are stored in this exhaustless reservoir of ethical energy. At such cost, my brothers, has Humanity issued this sacred book. From such patience of preparation has Providence laid this priceless gift before you. In such labor of articulation—spelling out the syllables of the message from on high, through multitudinous lives of men dutifully and devoutly walking with their God—does the Spirit speak to you, O, soul of man. Say thou—

Speak Lord; thy servant heareth!

It is a matter of perfect indifference where a thing originated; the only question is; Is it true in and for itself?

HEGEL: "Philosophy of History," Part III.: Sec. III.: Ch. II.

With reference to things in the Bible, the question whether they are genuine or spurious is odd enough. What is genuine but that which is truly excellent, which stands in harmony with the purest nature and reason, and which even now ministers to our highest development? What is spurious but the absurd and the hollow, which brings no fruit—at least, no good fruit.

GOETHE: "Conversations," March 11, 1832.

No article of faith is injured by allowing that there is no such positive proof, when or by whom these and some other books of holy Scripture were written, as to exclude all possibility of doubt and cavil.

WATSON'S "Apology for the Bible," Letter IV.

VI.

The Right Historical Use of the Bible.

The principle of development involves also the existence of a latent germ of being—a capacity or potentiality striving to realize itself . . . . What Spirit really strives for is the realization of its Ideal being. . . . .

The profoundest thought is connected with the personality of Christ—with the historical and external; and it is the very grandeur of the Christian religion that, with all this profundity, it is easy of comprehension by our consciousness in its outward aspect, while, at the same time, it summons us to penetrate deeper.

    HEGEL : "Philosophy of History," pp. 57, 344. [Bohn.]

Let mental culture go on advancing, let the natural sciences go on gaining in depth and breadth, and the human mind expand as it may, it will never go beyond the elevation and moral culture of Christianity as it glistens and shines forth in the gospel!

    GOETHE : "Conversations," March, 11, 1832.

VI.

The Right Historical Use of the Bible.

"When the fulness of the time was come God sent forth His Son."—GALATIANS, iv. 4.

ST. PAUL condensed the philosophy of Hebrew history into a metaphor. Israel travailed in birth with Christianity. In the mind of the nation was begotten, of the Most High, a conception of ethical religion, whose gestation was a process of centuries. The period of parturition came, and a universal religion was born into the world; bodied, as religion needs must be, in a man, Jesus, the Christ.

"When the fulness of the time was come God sent forth His Son."

The sacred literature of Israel is the record and embodiment of this organic growth of her religion, through its various moods and tenses, toward its ideal in the Christ. The sacred literature of the Christian Church is the picture of this flower of the soul of Israel, and of the new growth springing up from its seeding down of humanity. The whole Bible presents us with the growth of the religion of the Christ, below ground and above ground; its rootings and its flowerings. The right historical use of the Bible is, through a critical knowledge of the sacred literature of Israel, to reproduce before our minds this process of the growth of the Christ in Israel and of His new growth in humanity; with a view to our intelligent perception of His true place in history, and of the significance thereof. The heart of the Bible is Christ. That which our fathers saw we need to see, that in Him all things stand together, as the arch is holden by the key-stone. Rightly to read the secret of His life is to find the secret of earth's problems. Therefore our fathers insisted so strenuously on the Old Testament preparation for Christ. A tree's rootings are proportionate to its size. In the gradual prefiguring of Christ through Israel's story, they read the historic attestation of His revelation. The picture of Israel's history that yielded them their vision is dissolving before our eyes, at the touch of the new criticism, and men are fearing that the secret of the Bible is escaping from our age. I desire to-day to draw for you, in outline, the story of Israel's development, as traced by our new masters; that you may see the old vision re-emergent in truer, nobler forms. The re-construction of Hebrew history makes real and certain an organic, natural development of the religion of the Christ; a travail of the nation with the Son it bore to God.

The best method of studying any history is in its great epochs and periods. The eras of Hebrew history group themselves clearly, in orderly progression.

I.

The Epoch of Moses : B. C. 1300 (?)

Hebrew history properly begins with this era. The tribes of Israel when first resolved by the glass of history, appear upon the Arabian border of Egypt, as occupants of the rich pasture lands of Goshen. They were a branch of a large Semitic family, which included Moab, Edom, Ammon and other familiar tribes. Of the social, intellectual and religious status of the Hebrews at this period we have little definite information. They would seem to have been on the usual plane of races which have entered the semi-nomadic stage, and which are gradually substituting agricultural pursuits for a roving shepherd life. Oppressed by Egypt they revolt, and begin a migration backward toward the north and east.

The soul of this movement was Moses; a real historic figure, worthy, as we can see through the mists around him, of the imposing form which Michael Angelo has given him. A great man is nearly always to be found at the core of a great social growth, charging the latent tendencies of a race with energy, and shaping their action upon the form of his mind. "An institution is the lengthened shadow of a man," writes Emerson. Judaism is the lengthened shadow of Moses. Whatever else Moses may have done, he proved himself the architect of Israel, by laying the foundation that determined the form and size of the later structure. He taught his simple people to recognize Jehovah as their tribal God. What this name meant in the conception of the people before his time is by no means clear to us now. It appears to have stood for the personification of some one of the forms of nature's forces, that arrest upon themselves the nomad's vague sense of the Infinite and Divine in the world about him. Around the Power felt in Saturn or the Sun, Moses threw the spell of an awe which is deeper far than that awakened by the starry heavens above man—the awe aroused by the moral law within man. He gave his rude children a noble moral code, the original form of the Decalogue. These Ten Words were issued as the law of Jehovah. Jehovah then was the source and authority of the laws which the conscience owned. The moral law was his body of statutes. To keep this law was the way to please Him. His commands reached through rites and ordinances to conduct and character. His demands were not for sacrifices, but for good lives. His worship was aspiration and endeavor after goodness.

And this Power enjoining morality was none other than the Power which in nature seemed so often unmoral and even immoral. Jehovah of the skies was the God of the Ten Words.

This was a seminal thought, bodied in an institution. In begetting this conception in the soul of Israel, Moses fathered the life which grew through embryonic forms, during the slow gestation of the centuries, shaping toward the ideal of religion. Whatever was vital and progressive in the nation's thought and feeling sucked up its juices from the seed deep-rooted in this basic institution. Rightly did legislators and historians, through the after ages, look back and ascribe all their work in the development of the national life to Moses. Even thus the rose, were it conscious, might turn its crimson face upon the ground and whisper to the seed at its roots—I am thy work. Even thus the son, in the pride and power of manhood, goes back to the old homestead, and looking into his father's face confesses—All that I am you have made me.

II.

The heroic age: B. C. 1300–1100.

After Moses there follows a period of at least two hundred years, of which we have very imperfect accounts, and those plainly traditional and commingled with legend. The Hebrew tribes appear to have gradually gravitated upon Canaan; slowly settling into agricultural pursuits, and winning from its previous occupants the land they coveted, inch by inch, in bloody strife. They camped upon their hard-won fields for several generations, maintaining their claims at the point of the sword, with varying success; now mastering their foes, and again almost crushed by them. The inter-relations of the several tribes during this period would seem to have been of a very loose character. Each appears to have acted for itself, except at critical moments, when common danger drew them together in concerted action under leaders of commanding ability. Tradition has preserved charming tales of some of these redoubtable champions of the Hebrews, of whom we would gladly know much more. This was the heroic age of Israel. Rude, rough times of constant alarm brought forth little that was memorable save feats of courage. We have few glimpses into the state of religion in this simple society, and upon what is brought out into light the hues of later ages are reflected. Quite clearly we may discern that the religion of the people in those days was by no means that which we know as Mosaism. How could such a sublime conception as that of Moses have ripened in a people at this stage of their development? Like all founders of religion, he was far in advance of his age. If a few higher natures, here and there, recognized and appreciated the significance of the Ten Words of Jehovah, the mass of the people could not have done so. And movement is determined toward the mass in ethics as in physics. All that Moses could have hoped to do was to body his seminal truth in an institution, that should keep it alive in the nation until the proper conditions were found for its quickening and growth. This he achieved in binding the tribes to the worship of Jehovah, whose law was owned in the moral standards of the people. To this loyalty to Jehovah, as *the* God of Israel, Moses did securely bind the tribes. They never wholly forswore Jehovah, and thus never lost the germ begotten in the soul of the race, which held the promise and potency of the future.

But around Jehovah, as the supreme God of the race, the people still continued to group their ancient divinities, and to worship them in the old-time manner. The religion of a people in any stage of its history is always a composite; a succession of layers that correspond to the intellectual and moral classifications of society. But the proportion of the true religion rises with a progressive civilization. In these semi-civilized tribes the religion of the bulk of the people, in all probability, corresponded with the ideas and forms of worship of other peoples in the same stage of development. In the lowest stratum fetichism lingered on, the worship of any unusual thing that excited the wonder of a simple people. Great trees of immemorial age, huge boulders standing strangely in fertile valleys, continued the objects of superstitious awe. Jehovahism took up these remnants of fetichism into its higher life, when it found that they could not be dispossessed, just as Christianity did long afterward with pagan customs, and gave them a higher significance in connection with the worship of Jehovah.*

Higher strata of the people worshipped the various powers of nature, the sun, the moon, the stars, after much the same fashion in vogue among their kindred Semites.† Even the revolting rites of the surrounding nature-worships were not lacking in Israel. While the gentle and gracious warmth of the spring sun called forth the happy adoration of the people, the scorching and consuming heat of the midsummer sun roused the fears of the sufferers for their crops, their cattle, and their very lives. They sought to propitiate this fierce Power, which was evidently hostile to man, with offerings of the life it devoured so pitilessly. The choicest lives—the first-born son, the fairest maiden of the village—were sacrificed to glut its greed of death. Into the fiery arms of Moloch parents laid the children of their love. Human sacrifices were unquestionably a recognized form of worship during this period, at least in times of deep

---

* Of this process we see hints in the various references to the consecration of great trees and stones to Jehovah.

† The indications of this nature-worship lie scattered on the surface of the Old Testament so plainly that no one can fail to notice them.

distress.* The libertine longings of nature, the free fecundities of mother-earth, imaged to the grosser people the Power working round about them and within their very bodies; and men and women gave free rein to their appetites and passions, in honor of divinities like Ashera, the Syrian Venus.† The various tribes probably had different rites.

The general picture we must fashion in our minds of this period is of a polytheistic, idolatrous people, slightly distinguishable from the surrounding Semites, save as they held, in their recognition of Jehovah and his Ten Words, the germ of a higher thought and life.

---

* "Among the Edomites, Ishmaelites, Ammonites and Moabites—the tribes with which Israel felt itself most nearly related—the service of the rigorous and destroying god was most prominent. The very names for God which are most common among them—Baal, El, Molech, Milcom, Chemosh—are enough to show this. These names denote the mighty, violent, death-dealing God." "The Religion of Israel," Knappert, p. 29. These names constantly recur in the early history of Israel. Jephthah's vow is a familiar instance of this abhorrent rite. Circumcision is supposed to mark a merciful compromise with this blood-gift; in addition to its sanitary character.

†.We know from general history how among other people the homage paid to the productive powers of nature led to systematized prostitution, in the name of the personification of this force of nature. Tradition records how early in this period the Midianites seduced Israel temporarily from Jehovah, by the licentious pleasures of their worship of Baal-Peor. Later on in history we find that it is these impure rites that especially provoke the anger of the prophets.

III.

The period of the monarchy, down to the epoch of the great prophets : B. C. 1100–800.

The story of the making of England may interpret to us the development that ensued in this third period of Israel's history. We know how the petty realms of the Angles-land, under pressure from a common foe, learned to act momentarily together, came for a summer under some commanding leader, drew thus into closer affiliations, grouped gradually around the more powerful realms, and at length crystallized into England. In some such way the Hebrew tribes were slowly knit together by the necessity of war, until to organize a lasting victory they were forced into consolidation, and out of the loose confederation of tribes arose a nation, Israel. Social tendencies generally throw a leader to the front. The man is not wanting for the hour. The king-maker of Israel was Samuel. A man combining in that simple state of society several functions—priest and judge and leader—he had the prescience to divine the need of the age, and the wisdom to point out the man to meet it. Saul was chosen King, in free gathering of the hardy yeomanry, and proved his human election a divine selection by rousing the nation to new efforts, which his genius led to victory. Saul was followed by a brief period of national unity under David and Solomon, in which the rapid and brilliant progress made in the spread of the kingdom, in wealth and civilization, revealed the latent powers of this gifted race.

The progress of political and commercial greatness was stayed by the rending of the kingdom after Solomon. No great advances were possible amid the chronic jealousies and frequent strife of the sister kingdoms, which were unable to come together again in a unity that would have restored their prestige, and were unable, apart, to achieve any signal success in diplomacy or war.

The social state of the people underwent the changes usual in this stage of a people's history. With peace came wealth, with wealth came luxury, with luxury new social vices, fed from the court which grew around the monarchy. But that the heart of the people continued sound amid these organic changes we may see from several hints preserved by tradition.

The institution, or revival, of the Order of the Nazarites was a religio-moral movement. It was a protest against the vice of drunkenness that was increasing in the land, as, relieved from war's alarms and waxing fat upon their fertile fields, he people gave themselves to pleasure. The first Prohibition Society, of which we have record, was this Order of the Nazarites. This Order appears also to have had a still deeper moral aim, little noticed of old. It was a reaction from the social changes that were going on in Israel, a protest against the new-fashioned ways of wealth, an earnest effort to hold to the simplicities of earlier days, to the good old plain living and high thinking. It was a counter-movement of Old Israel, essaying to stem the mad rush for riches. A still more convincing token of the healthy moral tone of the nation is to be found in the earliest considerable work of literature preserved to us, the Song of Songs. It holds up to scorn the licentiousness that Solomon had made fashionable, and of which, in a just retribution, he had become the abhorred type. The great king fails to corrupt the virtue of a simple country maiden, despite of all his blandishments. Ewald assigns this poem to the northern kingdom, which had separated itself from Judah chiefly in reaction from the Solomonic innovations. It leads us into the homes of the sturdy peasantry of the hill country, where burned the fires on the altars of pure wedded love.

From a people thus sound at heart, amid the mellowing richness of civilization, we may well expect great things in religion. Whatever the outward forms of religion, its roots ran deep down into the moral law, and must needs have borne in due time a noble fruitage. There was in fact a striking development of religion in this period. It was coincident with the secular development of the nation. This indeed is the general rule of religious revival. Religion advances with the advancing life of man, each new and true step forward opening a higher possibility of thought and feeling concerning God. As Moses the Emancipator was the father of true religion in Israel, so Samuel the king-maker was its early master. We cannot now trace clearly his work, but we can see that he was a fresh ethical and spiritual force, shaping religious life anew.

Prophets there had doubtless been before him, in Israel as out of it, but they were unethical and unspiritual influences in religion; the frenzied dervishes, the oracular seers, the wizards and necromancers who long afterward claimed this name, and were denounced by the higher prophets. Samuel's masterful work was to turn this semi-religious force into a higher channel, and to direct it toward a moral aim. He was the creator of the type which drew after him "the goodly fellowship of the prophets." The traditions of Israel present him in the *rôle* of fearless censor and truthful mentor to the infant State; the *rôle* which the great prophets later on assumed toward the maturer nation. He criticized the King, guided the people, and held the nation loyal to Jehovah. However little perception the mass of the people had of the spiritual significance of the State religion, however many gross forms of popular religion existed around and within the tolerant institutions of Jehovahism, it was a vital matter to preserve that State religion, and keep it well ahead of the people's growth. Thus we can perceive the historic significance of the work of the next great prophet after Samuel, Elijah; through the legendary nimbus that gathered round his striking personality and dramatic action. In a critical hour, when the Jehovah-worship had well nigh disappeared, he stood alone against the powers of the realm, and rallied the people once more beneath the name of the god of their father. He plucked a victory from defeat which decided the course of history. What if Jehovah was but a name to the mass of the people? What if they continued to worship much as before, only no longer at the altars of Baal? There are long periods in the history of man when the future depends upon allegiance to an institution little understood by those who shout most lustily for it. The future may lie seeded down in a name which stores within it the forces of a new and higher unfolding, when the times come ripe. Thus it proved through the crawling centuries in which Israel held hard by a name of God which then meant little to it, but which ultimately evolved its ethical significance and manifested unto men, The Eternal who loveth righteousness. Thus may it prove with the child of Judaism. Liberals, who are in such haste to drop the name of Christ, should pause long enough to ask themselves the question whether, since it roots religion in a life of such perfect goodness that it became to men the manifestation of God, this sacred name may not in its turn hold the secret of our progress; whether, from the treasured forces of the past that it gathers into itself, when the spring time now setting in shall have fully come, it may not blossom into the religion of the future? A civilization should not be cut off from the historic seed which lies at the roots of its religion, if it is to grow unto the harvest.

That in this fidelity to the tradition of their race the religion of the people of Israel was in the vital processes of growth, through this long period, we know assuredly from one conclusive fact. Out of this tedious winter came, suddenly as it seems to us, a rich and beautiful spring. The epoch of the great prophets, with a new life of thought and aspiration, breaks in abruptly on this commingling of all sorts of religion within the precincts of Jehovahism. Even in February the sap is softening and warming in the veins which show no greening on the tips of the patient trees. Israel was swelling toward the day that was sure to come, when, lo! the spring!

IV.

The era of the great prophets, before the exile: B.C. 800–586.

In the southern Pacific, where coral islands are slowly forming beneath the surface of the sea, he who is curious to study the process of the making of an island must send the divers down to bring up broken bits of coral, snatched from the dark depths in a painful labor. After the ocean mountain thrusts its top above the surface of the sea the work of exploration is easy enough, and we may walk over hard ground as we study the new formation in the sunlight. Hitherto, in our desire to learn the secrets of the growth of Israel, we have been like men peering over the sides of their tiny boats into the depths of a sea that covers fascinating mysteries; watching the labors of the adepts who ever and anon bring up to the light some fresh fragments of a buried world. In the epoch that we have now reached Israel's growing life lifts itself above the level of tradition, and stands forth as solid history, on whose firm ground we can study for ourselves the making of a nation's religion.

Israel's literary period opens for us with the prophets. Literary fragments float up to us from earlier days, but now, for the first time, we have whole books about whose date and authorship we are reasonably certain. The prophets introduced the literary craft. They wrote out, in their later years, the substance of the messages which they had borne the people. These brilliant pages teem with graphic descriptions of the actual usages, social and religious, of their age, so that there is no difficulty in reproducing with fair accuracy the salient features of the period.

The popular religion was that composite of heathenisms already sketched in considering the previous period. The people continued to worship the Power which all felt and owned, under the manifold forms which this Power assumes in nature's processes. Sun and moon and stars still arrested the awe which through them groped after God, and drew upon themselves the worship of the imagination. The worship of Jehovah had a special honor as the State religion, but it stood contentedly amid other forms of religion. In the service of Jehovah local shrines developed special usages. The "Uses" of Israel were as varied as the "Uses" of England before the Reformation. No act of Uniformity was in operation in the realm. Idolatry was not the exception but the rule. The most popular symbol of Jehovah was an image of a bull. To the higher minds this bull was doubtless merely a symbol, expressive of a striking phase of the sun's force, but to the mass of men it was probably the actual object of their adorations. The symbolism of the Jerusalem Temple was thoroughly idolatrous; as, for example, the twelve oxen upholding the laver, and the horns of the altar, symbols drawn from the prevalent bull-worship; the two columns in the court, and the cherubs, or cloud-dragons in the most holy place; the *chamanim*, or sun-images, representing the rays of the sun in the shape of a cone, and the chariots and horses of the sun, a very ancient symbol familiar to us in Guido's Aurora.*

Nor did the allegiance to Jehovah bar private usages of an idolatrous nature. The home of the average Israelite had its *teraphim* and other domestic divinities. The darker aspects of the popular religion still held their ground against the growing light. Beneath the shadow of the Jehovah of the Ten Words, stood, unmolested, the images fashioned by the appetites and passions; and men and women surrendered themselves to drunken orgies and sensual debauches, in honor of the deities of desire. As late as the time of Jeremiah, after nearly two centuries of prophetic teaching, there were in the sacred precincts of the temple the *asheras*, or tree-poles, by which the priestesses of passion, as part of their religious offices, sold themselves to the frequenters of Jehovah's house.† Below the holy city, King Manasseh reared the image of Moloch, and human sacrifices were offered to placate the wrath of the Power which they ignorantly worshipped.

Where religion was so largely a worship of the physical powers of nature, the life of the people would of necessity show an undeveloped ethical

---

* The sun symbols may not have been permanent features of the Temple-worship at this period, though, from the probable identification of the early Jehovah with the sun, it seems likely that their presence there was no casual fact.

† 2 Kings, xxiii. 6, 7.

state. Drunkenness and debauchery continued common, the marriage bond was very elastic in the polite society of the capital, and selfishness haughtily overrode all considerations of *meum* and *tuum* in the mad chase of wealth.

Unsatisfactory as the morals of the influential classes of society were, there is, however, no indication of any such "ooze and thaw of wrong" as indicated a moribund condition in the nation.

We must not make the mistake, so common concerning reformers, and regard the evils that were justly lashed by the prophets as prevailing throughout society. Had this been the case, where would the ethical forces of a new and higher life have risen? Single preachers of social righteousness might have arisen, like Savonarola in Florence, under such conditions, but no general reform could have developed. The steady growth of the movement initiated by the great prophets shows that it sprang from no individuals, but from society; that they merely led the reserve forces of virtue in the nation. The heart of the nation was doubtless sound, and growing more vigorously virtuous. Professor Thorold Rogers reminds us that the period when a great outcry is heard against any social evil, is not that wherein the evil is at its height, for then there would probably be no power of protest, but rather that in which the recuperative forces of society are rallying to throw off the disorder from the body politic. Morality was in advance of religion at this time in Israel, and this interprets the movement which ensued to place religion in its proper position at the head of the march of progress.

It was amid such a state of affairs that the great prophets appeared upon the stage of action, calling the nation to a higher religion. They were not so much philosophers, reasoning out a lofty intellectual conception of God, as preachers of righteousness, vitalizing from the moral nature the sense of the purity and justice of the Power in whom men lived and moved and had their being. They turned the light of the inward law upon God, and revealed Him as its author. They led Virtue into the Temple, touched her lips with a live coal from off the altar, and from a tongue of fire men heard, "Thus saith the Lord." They revived the true Mosaic priesthood, which set apart conscience as the mediator between God and man. The seed that Moses planted budded and swelled toward its bloom. The prophetic writings show us men a-hungered after righteousness, breathing out the worship of Jehovah into the worship of the Eternal, who loveth righteousness.

Isaiah carries this message from God:

> To what purpose is the multitude of your sacrifices unto me?
> I am full of the burnt offerings of rams, and the fat of fed beasts.

THE RIGHT HISTORICAL USE OF THE BIBLE. 189

And I delight not in the blood of bullocks, or of lambs, or of he-goats.
When ye come to appear before me,
Who hath required this at your hand, to tread my courts?
Bring no more vain oblations;
Incense is an abomination unto me;
The new moons and Sabbaths, the calling of assemblies, I cannot endure;
It is iniquity, even the solemn meeting.
Your new moons and your appointed feasts my soul hateth;
They are a trouble unto me;
I am weary to bear them.
And when ye spread forth your hands,
I will hide mine eyes from you:
Yea, when ye make many prayers, I will not hear:
Your hands are full of blood.
Wash you, make you clean;
Put away the evil of your doings from before mine eyes:
Cease to do evil; learn to do well:
Seek judgment, relieve the oppressed,
Judge the fatherless, plead for the widow.*

Micah voices the questions that men raised in his day, answering them with the new thought:

Wherewithal shall I come before the Lord,
And bow myself before the high God?
Shall I come before him with burnt offerings,
With calves of a year old?
Will the Lord be pleased with thousands of rams,
Or with ten thousands of rivers of oil?
Shall I give my first born for my transgression,
The fruit of my body for the sin of my soul?
He hath showed thee, O man, what is good,
And what doth the Lord require of thee,

---

* Isaiah, i. 11–17.

> But to do justly, and to love mercy,
> And to walk humbly with thy God ?*

Two features of the work of the prophets bring out clearly their ethical inspiration. Israel was at this period being drawn, for the first time, into the currents created by the strife of the mammoth empires of Assyria and Egypt, in whose maelstrom she at length went down. Public affairs were becoming matters of international relationship. The prophets threw themselves heartily into the national politics, standing between the party of Assyria and the party of Egypt, as independents, concerned with the interests of neither faction, but seeking to lift both sides above the shifting sands of policy upon the firm ground of principle. They sought to lead the nation to turn aside from its dazzling dream of a brilliant foreign policy to the humbler tasks of internal reform; to induce the State to busy itself with the labor of redressing civic disorders and of building a community of sober, pure, and just citizens, cultivating peace and equity with other peoples, and fearing God. They were preachers to the corporate conscience of Israel, and dealt with subjects which the modern pulpit effeminately shuns. In strains of pure and passionate patriotism, they delighted to vision before the people the ideal State and its ideal King; thus to lead the aspirations of the

---

* Micah, vi. 6-8.

nation to a higher ambition than martial prowess and diplomatic craft.

> The spirit of the Lord shall rest upon him,
> The spirit of wisdom and understanding,
> The spirit of counsel and might,
> The spirit of knowledge and of the fear of the Lord;
> And shall make him of quick understanding in the fear of the Lord:
> And he shall not judge after the sight of his eyes,
> Neither reprove after the hearing of his ears:
> But with righteousness shall he judge the poor,
> And reprove with equity for the meek of the earth.
> And he shall smite the earth with the rod of his mouth,
> And with the breath of his lips shall he slay the wicked.
> And righteousness shall be the girdle of his loins,
> And faithfulness the girdle of his reins.*

These Hebrew prophets made the right administration of public affairs the essentially religious service which their devout student Gladstone declares them now to be. Because of this inspiration of civic life with religiousness, their books have become, as Coleridge called them, the Statesman's Manual.

At this period in Israel's history the social revolution attending the progress of all peoples from a simple to a complex organization was entailing its usual excesses, and alarming symptoms were showing themselves in the commonwealth. In earlier days Israel's tenure of land had been, like that of all peoples, communistic. Proprietorship

---

* Isaiah, xi. 2-5.

of the land was vested in the family, and then in the village community. There were no private fortunes and no private poverty. Life was simple, and contented, and dull. Under the action of the usual social forces, this system had been gradually breaking up, through many generations. Property had mainly passed into personal possession. Society had recrystallized around the individual. Individualism had developed its customary tendencies to inequality. The ancient equality of the free farmers of Israel was already disappearing. Fortunes, undreamed of a couple of centuries earlier, were becoming common. Greed was pushing men beyond legitimate acquisition into respectable robbery. The old-time rights of commonalty were disappearing in pasture, and farming land, and forest. The village commons were being "enclosed" by local potentates. Monopolies of the natural resources of all wealth, the inalienable dower of the people at large, were working their inevitable consequences. Below the wealthy class, which was rising to the top of society, there was forming at the bottom a new and unheard-of social stratum, the settlings of the struggle for existence; a deposit of the feebleness and ignorance and innocence of the people. In the loss of the old sense of a commonwealth, the nation was breaking up into classes, alienated, unsympathetic, hostile. Selfishness was threatening ruin to the State.

In the midst of these dangerous social tendencies the prophets came forward as "men of the people." Like brave Latimer at Paul's Cross, these fearless preachers stood in the market-places to denounce monopoly and the tyranny of capital. They were not affrighted by the hue and cry that, if human nature was the same then as now, was raised against them, in the name of the sacred rights of property. They were not beguiled by the sophisms of those who doubtless proved conclusively that the best interests of the people were being furthered by the fullest freedom of the able and crafty to enrich themselves *ad libitum*. They could not have stood an examination in political economy, but they knew the heart of the whole matter, in a world whose core is the moral law. They saw, more or less clearly, that there could be no lasting wealth in a society which was not based upon a wide, deep common-wealth. They felt that the one clue to follow in every social problem was held by conscience. So they struck boldly at existing wrongs in the name of the Eternal Righteous One.

> Woe unto them that join house to house,
> That lay field to field
> Till there be no place,
> That they may be placed alone in the midst of the earth !
> . . . . .
> The Lord will enter into judgment
> With the ancients of his people and the princes thereof:
> For ye have eaten up the vineyard ;

> The spoil of the poor is in your houses.
> What mean ye that ye beat my people to pieces,
> And grind the faces of the poor?
> Saith the Lord God of hosts.*

One word, constantly recurring through the prophets, reveals the secret of their enthusiasm. They lifted above the people the august and holy form of Justice, and called on men to follow her. They appealed to a force in men mightier than selfishness. They kindled the passion which had been always latent in Israel, since the day when Moses led forth the slaves of Egypt to found a nation of freemen. A new and lofty ideal mastered the minds of the better natures among the people. Over against the darkness of their age there rose a vision of a good time coming, when Justice should be throned on law, and selfishness be exorcised from the hearts of men who had learned the secret

> Of joy in widest commonalty spread.

And this they did in the name of Jehovah. From Him they came with these messages concerning social obligations. The Eternal One who loved righteousness could be served in no other way than in furthering justice. Religion became social reform, aflame with the enthusiasm of holy ideals; of ideals seen to be eternal realities, as the

---

* Isaiah, v. 8; iii. 14, 15.

shadows cast by The Living God, moving on to accomplish the good pleasure of His will.

To conserve the new spirit of brotherhood which they awakened, they embodied in the book of the Law, that constituted the Magna Charta of the Reformation, a development of a gracious usage of the people. From immemorial antiquity there had been a recognized right of the populace to the natural yield of the soil in every seventh year. This common law they formally re-enacted, in the name of Jehovah, and added to it a provision for the release of debtors in the sabbatical year.*

We shall see in the next period the fruitage of this new religion of social righteousness, in the remarkable legislation of the Restoration.

In these serious, strenuous secularities—so often neglected by the religious, or even opposed as irreligious—which now were consecrated to the service of Jehovah, religion found its true sphere, and developed its latent forces. A new era opened. The abominations of religion in former times became the exceptions rather than the rule, and gradually disappeared from society. After Jeremiah we hear no more of impurities hiding under the altar, or of savage superstition seeking to please Jehovah by outraging the holiest instincts of human nature. Jehovah became the name for a conception of Deity so spiritual, so

---

* Cf. Exodus, xxiii. 10, 11 (the earliest code) with Deuteronomy, xv. 1-18.

holy, that henceforth the student of Israel's history should substitute—God.

It is a most interesting study to place these great prophets in their chronological order, and trace the development of this ethical religion. As one after another they come upon the stage of action, they take up the great words of their masters and repeat them in their own way; take up the great tasks of their predecessors and carry them on toward completion; leading religion into an ever deepening spirituality. The prophets of the eighth century group around Isaiah, under whose influence Hezekiah attempted a partial reformation of the popular religion. The prophets of the seventh century group around Jeremiah, the master-spirit in the more thorough reformation carried out under Josiah. This second reformation achieved an institutional organization of ethical religion, that came just in time to create a body capable of holding the people together in loyalty to the true God, amid the break up of the nation.

v.

The Epoch of the Exile: B.C. 586–536.

The conquest of the two sister kingdoms, with the carrying away of the influential portion of the people into exile, was a blessing in disguise. Israel was taken out of its petty provincialisms, its race insularity, and placed amid one of the most highly cultivated civilizations of the ancient world. The fertile plain of Mesopotamia had been from immemorial antiquity the seat of great enterprises. Civilization had developed there when surrounding peoples had not emerged from semi-barbarism. Like the Troy beneath Troy in the Ilium ruins, we find here successive civilizations resting each upon the débris of an earlier order. The descriptions of ancient historians, together with the explorations of late years, make very vivid the scenes amid which the captive Israelites walked.

Babylon was a city which might well astonish and captivate strangers. It was of immense size, being surrounded by a wall forty, or possibly sixty, miles in circumference. This wall was nearly three hundred feet high, and was broad enough to allow a chariot with four horses to turn easily upon it. The streets were wide and straight, crossing each other at right angles, and were lined with houses several stories in height, painted in all the colors of the rainbow. Trees and gardens were so plentiful as to give the whole city the appearance of a park. The grounds of the imperial palace covered an area of seven miles round, in the centre of the city. The largest temple the world has ever seen rose in pyramidal form six hundred feet in air. The broad and shaded streets were resplendent with the pomp and pageantry of the court of a mighty empire, and were alive with the bustle of the traffic of the known world.

Libraries and museums garnered the treasures of art and literature, of science and philosophy, accumulated through centuries. On every hand were the tokens of a refined and cultivated civilization, venerable with age. In the temples a rich ritual celebrated an elaborate worship, while learned priests waited to explain the profound philosophic and poetic truths of the sacred symbols.

Transported to such surroundings, Israel received the mental shock which an American of a generation past experienced on first visiting Europe. The influence of this surprise was very marked. Israel's genius flowered in this strange soil. Her literary life centres in Babylonia. The second Isaiah wrote there his immortal pages. The unknown authors of the noble histories, whose charm never stales, fashioned there the traditions and records of the past into their present shape. There the great legal codification was carried out, and the institutional system of Israel perfected. A new circle of ideas show themselves at work in the mind of the people while in exile. From Chaldean scholars the Israelites probably learned the ancient legends of the Beginnings, which they worked over in their profounder religious consciousness into the simple and spiritual forms in which they stand in Genesis. From Persia they either received bodily the system of angelology that thenceforth appears in their writings, or they received the quickening influence of a kindred religion upon the thoughts latent in their beliefs.*

These intellectual influences wrought directly upon the development of Israel's religion. In the revelation of the prosperous life of these alien peoples, the chosen race saw herself but one member of the great world family. Persia's ethical and spiritual religion discovered to the nobler natures of Israel the very ideals which they and their fathers had long been strenuously seeking. These heathen were worshipping the same source and standard of goodness before which they themselves had been doing homage. A new sense of human brotherhood stirred within the exclusive race, and with it the perception that there is one Father of all men. Religion threw off all lingering polytheistic notions and soared to the vision of One God. Monotheism dates as a clear consciousness from this era.† It was saved from becoming an abstract, philosophic conception, merging good and evil in a common source, by the stern ethical dualism of the Persians. Though there be but one God, who is ultimately to triumph over all evil, yet, said

---

* The latter seems the probable influence of Persia. At all events, from this time Hebrew literature shows the gradual development of an angelic hierarchy.

† The comparison of the earlier prophetic writings with the exilic prophecies, and with the later writings, such as Jonah, Ecclesiastes, &c., will illustrate this change.

these Persians, evil is a present power in creation, organized and active, waging constant warfare with the powers of goodness. Earth is the scene of the battle between light and darkness, in which each man must play his part, for weal or for woe.

These high ethical and religious conceptions were nourished from the deeps of sorrow out of which the people cried bitterly to God. Their nation was crushed, their homes were broken up, and they themselves were captives in a strange land. Israel might have said,

> A deep distress hath humanized my soul.

All tender and gracious and holy humanities sprang forth from the hard Hebrew nature under this deep distress. The national ideal changed wholly. The old dream of a puissant king passed from the minds of the better men, and we hear little of it thenceforth in the writings of the nation. In the place of it arose the vision of the Righteous, Suffering, Servant of God—the Nation trained in the school of sorrow for a sacrificial mission, and charged to lead the peoples of the earth into the knowledge of the Eternal, who loveth righteousness.

As the crown and consummation of religion, the holy hope of life beyond the grave dawned in this night of suffering, gleaming toward the day of Him who brought life and immortality to light.*

---

* Ezekiel's vision of the valley of dry bones is the earliest ap-

Around this deepening and enriching life the remarkable body of the prophetic-priestly system was fashioned, as the law of the new nation when it should gain once more the old home. It looked to the formation of a holy people; through its minute direction of the daily life, its sacrificial symbolism charged with spiritual significances, its sacred books for the instruction of the people, its order of scribes devoted to this new study, its synagogues or meeting-houses for oral teaching and for prayer—now for the first time elevated into an act of public worship co-ordinate in dignity with sacrifice.

True to its old instinct, Israel's religion, first seeking to build up individual holiness, turned then to build up social righteousness. The ideals of the great prophets, which had been long working in the minds and hearts of the leaders of the people, were now embodied in the priestly legislation. The traditional communal system of land-holding was established as the legal basis for the new nation. The land of Israel was nationalized, and its title vested in God, from whom individuals received the right of limited usufruct. It could not be sold outright. No man could gain a fee-simple proprietorship. The seventh year was continued as a year of fallow, when the poor were to have the right of past-

---

pearance of this thought in any writing of whose date we are certain.

urage and of such growth as the land spontaneously brought forth. At the end of seven sabbatical periods, in round numbers every fifty years, all purchases of land were to lapse, and the soil return to the original possessors. At the same time all debtors were to pass through a general act of bankruptcy and go forth free men. Interest was not to be allowed on loans made between brother Israelites. By these provisions both villeinage or land-serfdom and the slavery of debtor classes to capital were to be prevented in the new nation. This legislation of the restoration was "to the end that there be no poor among you."*

---

* And thou shalt number seven sabbaths of years unto thee, seven times seven years; and the space of the seven sabbaths of years shall be unto thee forty and nine years. Then shalt thou cause the trumpet of the jubilee to sound on the tenth *day* of the seventh month, in the day of atonement shall ye make the trumpet sound throughout all your land. And ye shall hallow the fiftieth year, and proclaim liberty throughout *all* the land unto all the inhabitants thereof: it shall be a jubilee unto you; and ye shall return every man unto his possession, and ye shall return every man unto his family. A jubilee shall that fiftieth year be unto you: ye shall not sow, neither reap that which groweth of itself in it, nor gather *the grapes* in it of the vine undressed. For it *is* the jubilee; it shall be holy unto you: ye shall eat the increase thereof out of the field. In the year of this jubilee ye shall return every man unto his possession. And if thou sell ought unto thy neighbor, or buyest *ought* of thy neighbor's hand, ye shall not oppress one another: According to the number of years after the jubilee thou shalt buy of thy neighbor, *and* according unto the number of years of the fruits he shall sell unto thee: According to the multitude of years thou shalt

To such impracticable ideals, for that age, did this exilic movement of the new religion look,

---

increase the price thereof, and according to the fewness of years thou shalt diminish the price of it : for *according* to the number *of the years* of the fruits doth he sell unto thee. Ye shall not therefore oppress one another ; but thou shalt fear thy God : for I *am* the Lord your God.

* * * * * * * * *

The land shall not be sold for ever : for the land *is* mine ; for ye *are* strangers and sojourners with me. And in all the land of your possession ye shall grant a redemption for the land.

* * * * * * * * *

And if thy brother be waxen poor, and fallen in decay with thee ; then thou shalt relieve him : *yea, though he be* a stranger, or a sojourner ; that he may live with thee. Take thou no usury of him, or increase : but fear thy God ; that thy brother may live with thee. Thou shalt not give him thy money upon usury, nor lend him thy victuals for increase. I *am* the Lord your God, which brought you forth out of the land of Egypt, to give you the land of Canaan, *and* to be your God. And if thy brother *that dwelleth* by thee be waxen poor, and be sold unto thee ; thou shalt not compel him to serve as a bondservant : *But* as an hired servant, *and* as a sojourner, he shall be with thee, *and* shall serve thee unto the year of jubilee : And *then* shall he depart from thee, *both* he and his children with him, and shall return unto his own family, and unto the possession of his fathers shall he return. For they *are* my servants, which I brought forth out of the land of Egypt : they shall not be sold as bondmen. Thou shalt not rule over him with rigor ; but shalt fear thy God.— Leviticus, xxv. 8 *et seq.*

Fenton, "Early Hebrew Life," has, I think, given the clue through the difficulties of the jubilee-year legislation. He traces the early communal character of Hebrew society, its gradual break-up under the encroachments of manorial lords, and the natural efforts of the people to regain their communal rights. "But how remedy the evil ? How restore to the communities with sober, strenuous, systematic effort for their realization; and therein may we see its intensity of moral life.

VI.

The period of the Restoration, from B.C. 536.

The common notion is that this period of Israel's history was practically a vacuum, and that through five centuries the nation experienced no further development. In reality, it was an exceedingly active period, characterized by most important developments. Politically it was a period of constantly changing influences. Israel was scarcely ever really independent during these centuries. Her changes were the changes from one master to another. But this very subjection aided her intellectual development, as she was thus brought under the direct action of foreign ideas. Her

---

their old rights and privileges, without unduly trenching upon rights and possessions that had since been acquired? The year of Jubilee is the Hebrew solution of the problem," (p 71). It was a compromise; the old seventh year communal right adjourned to seven times seven years, and enlarged. Fenton quotes a curious survival, in the borough of Newtown-upon-Ayr, of this very compromise between the old and the new social systems—a Scottish Jubilee.

It is a queer sign of the disproportionate development of individual religion in our current Christianity, that this social and economic legislation should have been so spiritualized away as to leave no consciousness of its original character in the minds of those who sing in our prayer-meetings that " The year of Jubilee is come."

rapid growth of population forced upon her a system of emigration, that drew off her youth to the great centres of the world and established large colonies in every leading city. Israel was never left to settle down again into provincialism, but was stirred by the currents of the great world of thought that poured in upon her from Greece and Egypt, from Rome and the far East. "A cross-fertilization of ideas" was thus carried on by Providence. The result of grafting the richest varieties of thought upon such a sturdy stock could not fail of proving something rare and rich.

As was natural from such conditions, the thought of the nation took on new forms. Calm study of nature and man, and rational speculation on the great problems of life displaced impassioned and imaginative thought. Prophecy gave way to philosophy. The sages became the teachers of men. The third class of books in the Old Testament Canon, known by the Jews as the Writings, belong to this period; Proverbs, Ecclesiastes, Esther, Jonah, Daniel, etc. To this period also belongs the Apocrypha, which contains some noble books. These varied writings show, when critically studied, a direct bearing on the problems that we know were occupying the mind of the nation during this period, and illustrate the tendencies working among the people. We thus see, plainly, the growth of the seeds of noble thought which were sown in the national consciousness during the exile, and the growth of the rich germs wafted into Judea from Greece and Egypt.

We can trace the development of the circle of ideas which, later on, crystallized, under the ethical and spiritual force of Jesus into the theology of Christianity. We watch the embryonic stages of this thought-body, which at length awaited only the breathing within it of an informing spirit to issue in a new and noble religion.

Nor was this period of the Restoration merely one of intellectual development, else there would have been no such issue as came at length. It was a period of quiet ethical and spiritual development. No prophet arose, indeed, to quicken Israel, but the ancient prophets still spake from the institutions into which they had breathed somewhat of their spirit, and from the holy books which were read in every synagogue, and learned in every home. The temple worship of this period retained the old forms of sacrifice; but charged them with spiritual significances which are difficult for us to associate with such bloody rites, did we not know how easily the religious spirit adapts itself to any outward ceremonies, and transforms them into its own life. The soul spurns the symbols to which it yet will cling, and soars beyond the poor height to which the laboring wings of ordinance and ritual can carry it. The profound spiritual life which was awakened in the exile flooded these low forms with supernal light. They spoke to men of better sacrifices than the blood of bulls and lambs—of sins slaughtered and fleshly powers consumed, of lives of men offered up in purity to God. They whispered to the soul of the holiness of God, and of His forgiveness as well; and, in their powerlessness to satisfy the spiritual needs suggested by them, they kept men's eyes upon the future, looking for the Prophet greater than Moses, who would surely come from behind the veil with a new word from God. Out of such thoughts and feelings the temple worship drew upon itself a noble service of song, of whose ethical and spiritual beauty we can judge from the temple hymnal. You and I to-day have sung some of the very hymns which those Jews chanted around their brazen altar. Through these psalms of many ages, gathered into a hymnal of unrivalled nobleness, the worship of Israel ascended in the aspirations of the people after purity and righteousness. If the choirs sang of the Shepherd of Israel, it was not merely in the praises of the providential care felt over the chosen people, but in the thankfulness of souls, because of the assurance of His spiritual guidance:

He shall convert my soul,
And bring me forth in the paths of righteousness for His name's sake.

If they chanted the glories of the House of God, it was because thither the tribes came up, with this desire in the hearts of the worshippers:

> Like as the hart desireth the water-brooks,
> So longeth my soul after thee, O God.
> My soul is athirst for God. Yea, even for the living God:
> When shall I come to appear before the presence of God?
>
> . . . .
>
> O send out thy light and thy truth:
> Let them lead me;
> Let them bring me unto thy holy hill, and to thy tabernacles.
> Then will I go up unto the altar of God,
> Unto God, the gladness of my joy:
> Yea, upon the harp will I praise thee,
> O God, my God.

The temple, however, was but a part, and practically a small part, of the institutionalism of religion in this period. This was the era of the scribe rather than of the priest. Ezra came back to Jerusalem with a new treasure, "The Law." Around this sacred book, which soon added to itself the writings of the Prophets, the religious life of the nation really crystallized. To read and expound it, now that "no vision came to the prophets from The Eternal," became the highest office of religion, an office purely ethical and spiritual. In every town of the land the Meeting-house arose, opening its doors upon the Sabbath and on market days, to the villagers, who gathered for a simple service of instruction and devotion. The service began with a short prayer, which was followed by the recitation of some portions of "The Law," setting forth the great beliefs and duties of the Jewish religion—a confession of faith, in other words. After this came the long prayer, which, in later times, became liturgical; and then the reading of the lesson for the day from "The Law," with its interpretation, when Hebrew had become a dead language. Then followed a reading from the Prophecies, and a homily or sermon based upon the passage read. In their synagogues the Jews worshipped much as we are doing in this church to-day.

Through such a quiet deepening of the life of the people was the nation preparing for its final development of religion.

True it is that in the latter part of this period the nation showed unmistakable signs of being overtrained. The hedge made about the Law had fenced men off from one thing after another until, to men who were anxious not to offend, life became a weary burden. There was scarcely an action that might not involve sin. The natural effect of externalizing the commands of conscience followed; and the ethical aims which had been sought were well nigh lost in the routine of form and ceremony, and in the fine-spun distinctions of belief and conduct. A great-souled Jew found, later on, as hosts of his fellow-countrymen had found before him, that by the works of the Thorah (law or teaching) could no flesh be justified. The very Book which had fed so deep a life had come to stand between the soul and God, a barrier to the fresh, free inspirations from on high. Religion had run out upon the surface, and was dying. But it was as the tassels wither and whiten when the corn is ripe within the husk and ready to seed down a new season.

Plainly, by every sign, Israel's long gestation of Religion was nearing its appointed term. All the elements had been developed, one after another, for a Universal Religion, and there was nothing more to be done but to await the coming to the birth. As plainly, by every sign, the world-conditions were at length found for a safe issue of the "holy thing" which Israel so long had carried within her bosom. There was needed a man to body these scattered elements, to fuse the forces of the nation into a personality, to live the dreams which a race had visioned. Religion is never a code nor a theory, it is always a life. The ideal religion awaited the ideal man. He came! As the nation held the holy child Jesus in her arms, joying that a MAN was born into the world, she might have been overheard singing:

> Lord, now lettest thou thy servant depart in peace,
> According to thy word:
> For mine eyes have seen thy salvation,
> Which thou hast prepared before the face of all people;
> A light to lighten the Gentiles,
> And the glory of thy people Israel.

The historical reality of Jesus is unquestionable. The essential features of his life and thought are distinctly outlined through the mist of time, and above the clouds of legend that hang low upon the horizon where he disappeared. The threefold tradition preserves a clear-cut image of the Son of Man. We see One in whom the ideals of Israel found a perfect realization. He brought to the flower the conception of religion whose germ lay seeded down in the Ten Words of Moses. In him worship and aspiration were one. He lived the ethical and spiritual religion after which the nation had patiently striven, through prophet and priest and sage, through psalmist and through scribe. He *lived* the vision of human goodness which holy men of old had never succeeded in bringing down into the flesh, beyond a blurred blocking in of the heavenly ideal. He *lived* man's dream of goodness so gloriously that he became a more than man, in whom was felt the coming nigh of the Eternal Holy One. The human form divine, to which mankind aspired, took on its true and awful splendor, as the image of the God whom the conscience worshipped. Every passing "I would be," of the saints of old looked forth, transfigured, from the face of One who said "I AM."

True to Israel's ancient dream, around this righteous suffering servant of the Eternal, the nations gathered, to be taught of God. The souls to whom He gave power to become the sons of God became the family of the Heavenly Father, in which there was "neither Greek nor Jew, circumcision nor uncircumcision, Barbarian, Scythian, bond nor free, but Christ was all and in all." In this holy brotherhood of the children of the All-Father, we moderns take our places round our elder brother; feeling sure that we have found the spiritual band or religion wherein society is to be held together, through each man's holding hard by the God who is the perfection of His own highest dreams.

Such then being the fact of Israel's historic travail and such her issue, our fathers' sense of the supreme significance of Christ in human history takes on a new light in our new knowledge.

The problem of religion is to find such a knowledge of the Being in whom we live and move and have our being, as shall lead men's awe before this mysterious Power up into an awe of a Power whom we may rightly worship, trust and love. To find the key to this problem is to hold the secret of all the puzzles of our weary world. Before the Power "manifest in the flesh" in Jesus Christ, our souls hush, in an awe which breathes within us worship, trust and love. And if this Power be the very Power felt in history and in nature, whose ways therein are so often baffling to the moral sense, then all is well. But, if this be so, the holy Power who is shrined in Christ must show the features of the Mind which tabernacles in nature. There can be no contradiction. Unquestionably an essential characteristic of the

Mind in nature is the method of its action. There is a reign of Law. The highest generalization of the methods of this law which man has reached reveals this Power as acting, through every sphere, in continuous progressive development. One word embodies this supreme generalization—evolution. Christianity must fit into this universal order. Otherwise it either denies that order, which denial cannot be received; or it is denied by that order, which denial is very certain to be increasingly received. God "cannot deny Himself!" "I change not."

Here is where Christianity's hold of the human mind hinges in our age. The old reading of the history of the preparation for Christ separated "those whom God hath joined together" The new reading of that preparation restores the needful unity.

Christianity is no exception amid the general order of nature. It follows that providential plan. It grows from seed to flower. Its beginnings were in a simple conception of ethical religion begotten in a heathen people through Moses. In the womb of the nation it lay dormant till the time for quickening came. Thenceforward it slowly assimilated the vital forces and nutritive elements of the organic life within which it grew, until the hour arrived when it burst the maternal womb, a perfect birth. Christianity is a genuine historic evolution.

When we have said this, have we accounted for it? To none save those who, in mastering the methods of a process of evolution, fancy that they have mastered its sources. To none save those who, familiarizing themselves with the order of life, think that they have resolved its nature. The wiser portion of mankind do not find in How a synonym for Whence. We still ask whence? When we see the issue of a long and complicated plan, we postulate a planning mind. When we trace, through the sketches and studies in a studio, the gradual embodiment of a vision of loveliness, which at length looks down upon us in its perfect grace from the canvas on the wall, we cannot be persuaded out of our conviction that some artist has lived and labored in this studio, patiently evolving his great dream. When we see a new-born child we do not think that we have learned its parentage in being told about its mother. We want to know who fathered it into being.

What mind planned this process of a nation's growth into a universal religion? What artist dreamed this ethical and spiritual ideal? Who begat this "holy thing" conceived in Israel and born of her at length in glorious beauty? If Moses was the human parent of this marvellous child, who fathered the "essential Christ" in Moses? Who is the real father of Jesus Christ?

Our only answer must be that given of old:

THE RIGHT HISTORICAL USE OF THE BIBLE. 215

When the fulness of the time was come God sent forth His son. . . . . The true Light, which lighteth every man, was coming on into the world. . . . . And the Word became flesh and dwelt among us (and we beheld His glory, the glory as of the only-begotten of the Father) full of grace and truth.

If this then be the true interpretation of the evolution of the Christ, we hold, in the doctrine of the Incarnation, the secret of all evolution. We must read the story of every development in the light of the highest life of man, himself the highest life of nature. Nature is in travail with an ideal which rose not in the molten suns, though perchance it did rise through them.

The whole creation groaneth and travaileth in pain together until now. For the earnest expectation of the creature waiteth for the manifestation of the sons of God.

Man is in travail with an ideal which rose not in the anthropoid apes, though it may have risen through them. A finer, larger, nobler man is growing within the man that is.

The Universal Man is now coming to be a real being in the individual mind.

Mankind, which is one physically and mentally, is one morally and spiritually. All varieties of man are built upon one ethical type. The virtues are cosmopolitan. . One human ideal looms above and before all races, though refracted differently in the changing atmospheres of earth. Within the saints one dream of goodness forms.

Over the seers and sages one vision of the source of human goodness rises. Through the clouds of earth one Infinite and Eternal Form shapes itself to the wise. As men rise they meet. The race-souls are strangely alike. Socrates and Buddha are brothers. Humanity is in travail with one Human Ideal and one Divine Image, and these twain are one. The great Mother sings to herself:

> But he, the man-child glorious,
>   Where tarries he the while?
> The rainbow shines his harbinger,
>   The sunset gleams his smile.
>
> My boreal lights leap upward,
>   Forth right my planets roll,
> And still the man-child is not born,
>   The summit of the Whole.
>
> I travail in pain for him,
>   My creatures travail and wait;
> His couriers come by squadrons,
>   He comes not to the gate.

Will Humanity come to the birth with her beloved son? Who that reads the story of the coming of the Hebrew Christ can doubt it? What miscarriage can befall her who is nursed by Nature and tended by Providence? What will the Coming Man be like? We have seen his face break through the flesh for a moment. On the shoulders of the race will rest the head of Christ. What shall be said when the morning stars sing together, and all the sons of God shout for joy that MAN is born upon the earth?

> The Holy Ghost hath come upon thee, Humanity, and the power of the Highest hath overshadowed thee; therefore also, that holy thing which is born of thee, shall be called the SON OF GOD.

This, at least, is my reading of nature and of history in the light of the completed evolution of the Christ. The normal growth through history of the Ideal Man, is the incarnation of the Divine Man. The mischievous antithesis between the realms of the natural and the supernatural, that kept the world's thought from crystallizing around the world's soul, disappears in an Order which is at once natural in all its processes, and supernatural in its source and plan and energy.

We hold the key to all earth's problems in the vision of God which, gleaming through nature and through man, dawns in the face of Jesus Christ. Over Him—in whom the Human Ideal becomes the Divine Image, and the most perfect dream of human goodness is the revelation of earth's God—the Eternal One breaks silence, whispering to our souls:

> This is my Beloved Son: Hear Him!

VII.

The Right Ethical and Spiritual Use of the Bible.

It is impossible to forget the noble enthusiasm with which this dangerous heretic, as he was regarded in England, grasped the small Greek Testament which he had in his hand as we entered, and said: " In this little book is contained all the wisdom of the world."

     STANLEY: "History of the Jewish Church," III. x.
     [Reminiscence of a visit to Ewald.]

Truth, not eloquence, is to be sought for in Holy Scripture. We should rather search after our profit in the Scriptures, than subtilty of speech. . . . . Search not who spoke this or that, but mark what is spoken.

     À KEMPIS : " Imitation of Christ," Ch. V.

Do not hear for any other end but to become better in your life, and to be instructed in every good work, and to increase in the love and service of God.

     JEREMY TAYLOR: "Holy Living," Ch. IV. Sect. iv.

> We search the world for truth : we cull
> The good, the pure, the beautiful
> From graven stone and written scroll,
> From all old flower-fields of the soul ;
> And, weary seekers of the best,
> We come back laden from our quest,
> To find that all the sages said,
> Is in the Book our mothers read.
>
>   WHITTIER : "Miriam."

VII.

The Right Ethical and Spiritual Use of the Bible.

"From a child thou hast known the Holy Scriptures, which are able to make thee wise unto salvation through faith which is in Christ Jesus."—2 TIMOTHY, iii. 15.

THE right use of the Bible is admirably stated by St. Paul. These books do not make one learned in any knowledge—they make one wise in life. The Jewish tradition concerning Solomon's choice expressed a deep truth. Wisdom is the supreme benediction to be sought in life. Invaluable as is knowledge, it is as a means to an end. Knowledge provides for man the material out of which Wisdom, using "the best means to attain the best ends," builds a noble life. To have the mind clear, the judgment just, the conscience true, the will strong, so that we may sight the goal of life, may learn the laws by which it is to be won, and may firmly seek it, steadfast amid all seductions—this is wisdom.

Would that for one single day, we may have lived in this world as we ought.

Thus prays the author of the Imitation of Christ; and in so praying he is sighing after wisdom.

This culture of wisdom is the aim of the books which together form the Bible. They reveal to our vision the best ends in life, and point us to the best means of winning those high aims. They clear the atmosphere of mists, disclose to us our bearings, and fill our souls with the afflatus which wafts us toward "the haven where we would be." These books are rightly called by Paul, the "Holy Scriptures," the scriptures of holiness, the writings whose genius is goodness. Their charm is "the beauty of holiness," the graciousness of Goodness as she unveils herself therein. And this genius of gracious Goodness which irradiates the inner court of this temple, lays such a spell upon the souls of men inasmuc has she is seen to be the very daughter of God; according to the soliloquy overheard by mortal ears, wherein Wisdom sings:

> The Lord possessed me in the beginning of His way,
> Before His work of old.
> . . . .
> Then I was by Him, as one brought up with Him,
> And I was daily His delight, rejoicing always before Him.

Religion becomes the worship of the God who is the source and standard of goodness, the love of the Eternal who loveth righteousness, the child's crying out into the dark—O righteous Father.

> The fear of the Lord is the beginning of Wisdom.

The Bible is the choicest extant literature of

the people of religion, the record and embodiment of the evolution of ethical worship, through its varied moods and tenses, into its perfect type in Jesus Christ our Lord. The Bible-books form, therefore, the classics of the soul, in which we are to study the nature and secret of goodness; the manual which every earnest man and woman, intent on building character, should use habitually for ethical culture, and for the ethical worship which is its inspiration. This is the truest use of the Bible.

The intellectual use of the Bible, in critical and historical studies, is legitimate and needful. Reason should lay the bases for faith. Knowledge must rear the altar on which worship is to be lighted. Theology shapes religion. It is all important, therefore, that the books which the intellect chiefly uses to found and form its thoughts of God should be rightly used, so as to give man right conceptions of the Divine Being, and to waken right feelings toward Him. This intellectual use of the Bible is not for scholars alone. There is no longer any isolated class of scholars. All educated people are now taken into the confidence of the learned, in every sphere of knowledge. The average man will reason about the great mysteries quite as much as the scholar; perhaps more than the true scholar, and with more insistent dogmatism. To the issue of that simpler, nobler Religion of Christ which is struggling to the birth within the womb of Christianity, in the travail throes that are upon our age, it is of vital moment that all intelligent people should learn to use their Bibles intelligently; in a knowledge of the nature of its writings, and in reasonable reasonings therefrom. Therefore I have spoken concerning the critical and the historical uses of these sacred writings.

But, when this knowledge is won and duly employed in our theologizings, the truest use of the Bible remains for us to make, to our highest pleasure and profit. It is the book of religion, not of theology; save as it records the one authoritative Epistle of Theology, the Word of God, the Christ. It is not a body of divinity, it is the soul of divinity. To use the Bible critically and historically for our theologizings, is, after all, to use it, however rightly, for its secondary and not its primary purpose. Religion—as the awed sense of the Eternal Power and Order revealed in nature, the Infinite Goodness and Righteousness revealed in man—is the art of the soul; its finest feelings, its loftiest imaginations, its noblest enthusiasms, its profoundest tragedies thrown out into the cry of the human after God.

There is a science in the sculptor's art. It is doubtless needful that this art should be studied for the sake of its science. Artists, however, may be glad that Winckelmann has analyzed the Apollo Belvedere, and has given them the laws of proportion deduced from this human form divine; leaving them free to feast upon its beauty. For in the scientific study of art, art itself may be lost. Some great figure-painters have been unwilling that their pupils should study anatomy; fearing that the bones would stick through the flesh in their paintings.

This danger shows itself plainly in all critical and historical uses of the Bible, in the old-fashioned as in the new-fashioned study of the Bible.

The international series of Sunday-school lessons burden the brief hours of the Lord's Day with a mass of matter, which may or may not be true knowledge about the Bible, but which certainly is not the true religion of the Bible. A child may learn the tables of the Israelitish Kings, the geography of the Holy Land, and the architect's plans of the temple of Jerusalem, and may be learning nothing whatever of the real religion which is shrined within the Bible. That is very simple:

> Thou shalt love the Lord thy God with all thy heart, and with all thy mind, and with all thy strength: And thy neighbor as thyself.

The time spent on these more or less interesting matters may rob the child of his one weekly opportunity of learning to use the Holy Scriptures so as to become wise unto salvation. To use their words of wise men, and their tales of holy men, to inspire the love of goodness as the love of God, this and this alone is to teach religion from the

Bible. Bread that consists of two-thirds bran and one-third white flour is eminently laxative; but it is generally supposed that this age is lax enough in its hold of truth. A little more wheat and a little less bran, ye good doctors, might strengthen the constitutions of our children.

The new study of the Bible is perhaps even more in danger of missing its real secret. An interest in the literature and history of Israel may divert the mind from that which is, after all, the heart of these "letters," and the core of this history.

> Fear God and keep His commandments; for this is the whole duty of man.

Of this danger I think that I see signs, in some of the great masters to whom we owe our new criticism, in some of the manuals which are popularizing it, and in some of the gifted preachers who are reconstructing theology around it. The science of religion is absorbing too much of the life that should go into the art of religion; and we have fine forms of thought, mantled with flabby flesh of feeling, in which no red blood of holy passion pulses.

To read Homer with a view of understanding the fables of superstition, and of interpreting the mythology of the ancients, may have been needful for the later Greeks, who would preserve religion from the death that was stealing over it, in the divorce of the educated and the popular thought of the Grecian Bible. Such a use of Homer, however, must have missed the essential charm of Homer—the immortal poetry of these heroic legends; the breath of fresh, simple, wholesome human life which animates them, and which through them inspired men to brave and noble being. Socrates saw this in his day.

"I beseech you to tell me, Socrates," said Phaedrus, "do you believe this tale?" "The wise are doubtful," answered Socrates, "and I should not be singular if, like them, I also doubted. I might have a rational explanation. . . . Now I have certainly not time for such inquiries; shall I tell you why? I must first know myself, as the Delphian inscription says. To be curious about that which is not my business while I am still in ignorance of my own self, would be ridiculous." *

Wisely speaks the finest Biblical critic of England in our day:

No one knows the truth about the Bible who does not know how to enjoy the Bible; and he who takes legend for history, and who imagines Moses, or Isaiah, or David, or Paul, or Peter, or John, to have written Bible-books which they did not write, but who knows how to enjoy the Bible deeply, is nearer the truth about the Bible than the man who can pick it all to pieces but who cannot enjoy it. . . . His work is to learn to enjoy and turn to his benefit the Bible, as the Word of the Eternal.†

The right use of the Bible is to feed religion. Coleridge said:

---

* The Dialogues of Plato: Jowett's edition, II. 106.
† Matthew Arnold in *Contemporary Review*, xxiv. 800; xxv. 503.

Religion, in its widest sense, signifies the act and the habits of reverencing the invisible, as the highest both in ourselves and in nature.*

The use of the Bible then is to ennoble our ideals, to quicken our aspirations, to clear the illusions of the senses, to dissipate the glamor of the world, to purify our passions, to bring our powers well in hand to a firm will; and, through the mystic laws of nature and of conscience which we thus endeavor to obey, to breathe within our souls a sacred sense of the Presence of a Power, infinite and eternal and loving righteousness—whom to know "is life eternal."

De Quincey classified all writings as belonging either to the literature of knowledge, or the literature of power. There are books to which we go for information. They give us facts and ideas. They constitute the literature of knowledge. They teach us. There are books to which we go for inspiration; to which we turn for joy and pleasure, for strength and courage, for patience and endurance, for purity and peace. They constitute the literature of power. They move us. Herbert Spencer's books belong to the literature of knowledge. The "Imitation of Christ" belongs to the literature of power.

The literature of knowledge needs to be reissued every century or generation or decade, cor-

---

* The Friend: Essay x.

rected up to date. The literature of power is immortal; fresh to-day though born milleniums ago. The problems of character and conduct face us much as they faced the Romans and Greeks, the Egyptians and Hindus. The invisible in nature and in man touches us with the same feelings that it stirred in Persians, Chaldeans and Akkadians. Even though the Spirit's voice spake once in a language of the intellect which has now become obsolete, its utterances are not therefore obsolete. How archaic is much of the thought of the "Imitation of Christ;" shot through and through as it is with the tissue of mediæval Catholicism! But we forget these archaisms in the spell of a holy soul, in love with wisdom, "intoxicated with God." No archaisms in Biblical thought destroy its spiritual power over us. Nay, rather do they strengthen that power: as in our devotions we naturally seek old and quaint forms, buildings unlike other structures, music which sounds from out the past, words that are mellow with the rich hues of age; as the archaisms of the language of our English Bible hold a power that is lost in the raw correctness of the revised version.

In the literature of power the Bible ranks first. Whatever in Christian literature has most searching ethical and spiritual energy radiates the reflected light of the Bible. Augustine's Confessions, The Imitation of Christ, Fenelon's Spiritual Letters, The Saints' Rest, The Pilgrim's Progress, in their most appealing tones echo the voices of the Bible. The hymns that feed the inner life are aromatic with the rich thoughts and feelings of this holy book. Our poets betray, in the passages which are the favorites of earnest minds, the influence of these Scriptures. From Paradise Lost to In Memoriam, from The Temple to the Christian Year, the poems which the devout delight in are either Biblical paraphrases or Biblical distillations. Our masters of fiction could not have written the scenes which most rouse our moral nature, could not have conceived the characters which most inspire our devotional nature, without the Bible. Take the Bible out of Adam Bede and Dinah Morris, out of Robert Falconer and M. Myriel, the blessed Bishop of D., and what would be left of them? The vibratory quality which most thrills our souls in the strains of Christian literature is due to the Bible material in it. The Bible holds stored the ethical electricity on which Christendom has drawn, through centuries, exhaustless energy.

Outside of Christendom, while there are many books which we can thankfully and reverently place by the side of the Bible, as ethical and spiritual motors, there are none which any of us would think of substituting for it. The Discourses and the Manual of Epictetus, the Thoughts of Marcus Aurelius, the Dialogues of Plato, and the kindred words of wisdom of the ancients, are indeed full of inspiration to earnest natures. To dip into these writings for a few minutes, amid the duties of the day, is a soul bath, most cleansing and invigorating. The Sacred Books of the East may well be sacred to us Westerns. A sense of grateful awe steals over me as, looking on these volumes, I think of the generations which they have fed with spiritual sustenance and have guided in the way of life. The light which lighteth every man that cometh into the world shines through these pages. The All-Father has drawn nigh to the souls of His children, through the holy men who spake as they were moved of the Holy Ghost. It is an inestimable privilege to have these Bibles of Humanity ranged along our shelves, and to have their choicest words at hand upon our tables, in some apt anthology. It would be well if their great sayings could be read in our churches, in connection with our Old Testament lessons, as the voices of the ethnic prophets of the Son of Man. But if we have allowed the thought that any of these sacred books might become a substitute for our fathers' Bible, we may correct our crude enthusiasms by the authority of the greatest living master in Comparative Religion. In the preface to the edition of the Sacred Books of the East that noble monument of our generation's scholarship, Max Müller, writes:

Readers who have been led to believe that the Vedas of the

ancient Brahmans, the Avesta of the Zoroastrians, the Tripitaka of the Buddhists, the Kings of Confucius, or the Koran of Mohammed, are books full of primeval wisdom and religious enthusiasm, or at least of sound and simple moral teaching, will be disappointed on consulting these volumes. . . . I cannot help calling attention to the real mischief that has been done, and is still being done, by the enthusiasm of those pioneers who have opened the first avenues through the bewildering forest of the sacred literature of the East. They have raised expectations that cannot be fulfilled, fears also that, as will be easily seen, are unfounded. . . . I confess it has been for many years a problem to me, aye, and to a great extent is so still, how the Sacred Books of the East should, by the side of so much that is fresh, natural, simple, beautiful and true, contain so much that is not only unmeaning, artificial and silly, but even hideous and repellant. *

Our own Bible, as I have frankly owned, holds the truth as the gold is held in the ore. Truth nowhere exists "native" in human writings; but the proportions of the "mineralizer" are vastly greater in all other Bibles than in our own. There is no book known that can take its place on the lecterns in our churches, or on the tables by which, in quiet hours, we seat ourselves, a-hungered for the bread of life.

The pre-eminent excellence of Israel's writings in the literature of power, is natural and necessary. Israel had little originality in any science or art save the science and art of the soul, the knowledge and the love of God. Nature is economic in her dowries. She does not shower all the gifts of the

---

* Sacred Books of the East : I. ix. *et seq.*

fairies on any one race. She dowered Israel with the highest of human powers, conscience, in an unequalled measure. Providence nurtured and trained this faculty. This little nation became as pre-eminently the people of ethical and spiritual religion as the states of Greece became the people of art. Because of the natural aptitudes of Israel, and of her providential education, we should turn to her literature for our highest inspirations in ethical culture and religion.

I.

Wherein lies this commanding rank of the Bible in the literature of ethical and spiritual power?

Speaking generally, I should say that the superiority of the Bible lies in the fact that it is at once a literature of ethical power and a literature of spiritual power. We have books of high ethical power that are weak religiously. We have books of high religious power that are weak ethically. The Bible is strong in both directions. Hence its power. Either ethical or spiritual power alone is defective. Morality without spirituality is principle without passion. Spirituality without morality is passion without principle. Union supplements the defectiveness of each alone, and develops its full forcefulness. The Bible marries morality and spirituality, and these twain become one. The secularities become sacred, and the sanctities become sound.

According to the Bible, he who keeps the Ten Words obeys God. The "merely moral" man is a worshipper of God, though the worship may be silent. In Kant's great saying, They are always in the service of God whose actions are moral. Virtue becomes consciously religious, as she learns to recognize what she is in love with in loving goodness. As the love of goodness rises into a passion for the ideal forms of Justice, Purity and Truth, it takes on a real religiousness. It may think to stop short in an ethical culture, but it cannot. To feed its own aspirations it must worship the Ideal Righteousness as a reality. Its desires become prayers, its hopes become praises. Even though in mute longings, it pleads

O Lord, open thou our lips, and our mouth shall shew forth Thy praise.

Reversing the identification of religion with morality that is wrought by the Bible, its influence is equally impressive. Religion is not the emotion of man in the presence of the invisible in nature, unless that invisible is felt to be essentially moral. Religion is not the finest of feelings before the invisible in man, unless that unseen is also felt to be ethical. The Natural Religion, however nobly stated, which accepts any form of poetic ideals as religion, is very imperfect and not at all Biblical. Shelley's feelings for the spirit of Beauty are exquisitely fine, but under the light of the Bible they are seen to be only latently religious. A more penetrating vision will see in the Ideal Beauty a Moral Form, and then æsthetics will translate itself into ethics. The unmoral sentiment of a Shelley for Beauty may issue in another generation in the immoral sentiment of a Swinburne. Even thus the vision of the Aphrodite sank into the dream of a Venus. An Oscar Wilde's maunderings over an art which has no reference to morality may possibly be poetry, but they certainly are not religion according to the Bible, for all his blasphemous apostrophes to Christ between his praises of licentious love. Hard as the granitic core of earth is the core of religion in the Bible.

The "stern law-giver" of Israel was Duty. Her supreme authority, which enjoined with absolute command the most unpleasant action, was—"I ought." She saw that "laws mighty and brazen" bind man to a right, which he may distort or deny, but cannot destroy—his Saviour or his Judge. Mystic in its sacredness, Conscience sat shrined within the soul of the holy men who spake as they were moved of the Holy Ghost; her voice the very voice of God. The Power in whom we live and move and have our being is revealed in these books as the Eternal Righteousness. The moral law is seen to be the throne of the Most High.

In Emerson's phrase:

> Virtue is the adopting of this dictate of the Universal Mind by the individual will.

"What do I love when I love Thee?" sighed Augustine. Israel might have answered that question in Augustine's own words:

> Not the beauty of bodies, nor the fair harmony of time, nor the brightness of the light so gladsome to our eyes, nor sweet melodies of varied songs, nor the fragrant smell of flowers and ointments and spices, not manna and honey. None of these do I love when I love my God; and yet I love a kind of light, a kind of melody, a kind of fragrance, a kind of food, when I love my God,—the light, the melody, the fragrance, the food of the inner man. This it is which I love when I love my God.*

But the Bible answer would be much more simple and pungent:

> O ye that love the Lord, see that ye hate the thing which is evil.... If a man say I love God and hateth His brother he is a liar.

This is the fundamental secret of the power of the Bible. The love of goodness and the love of God are one. Aspiration is unconscious worship, and worship is aspiration conscious of its object.

> Be ye perfect as your Father which is in heaven is perfect.

But this noble conception of the unity of ethical and spiritual life has many aspects in the Bible. The Bible turns upon us every phase in which Wisdom reveals herself to the sons of men, so that no ray of her light is lost, and that every one, however he may stand related to her, receives her heavenly beams.

---

* Confessions of Augustine: Book X. § vi.

1. *We have here the simple, homely, prudential aspects of virtue, which have always been particularly powerful on certain ages and classes.*

The maxims of a Poor Richard are anticipated here, as quaint, as terse, and as sagacious in the ancient Jew as in the modern American. Our scientific teachers would replace eloquent declamation concerning vices, such as drunkenness and debauchery, by illustrated lectures upon the physiological effects of violations of nature's laws. They would teach men that the laws of health are found in the laws of temperance and purity. The Hebrew sages had this vision of Wisdom. Their proverbial sayings abound with graphic pen-pictures of the folly of vice. No illustration of the physical consequences of debauchery could be more impressive than the vivid sketch of the foolish young man, going after the strange woman as an "ox goeth to the slaughter," knowing not that

> Her house is the way to hell,
> Going down to the chambers of death.

The favorite name for sin in these proverbs is Folly. Wisdom crieth to the sons of men, in that noblest writing of the sages:

> Blessed is the man that heareth me,
> Watching daily at my gates,
> Waiting at the posts of my doors.
> For whoso findeth me findeth life,
> And shall obtain favor of the Lord.

But he that sinneth against me wrongeth his own soul.
All they that hate me love death.

2. *These laws of life that work for our health and wealth loom, however, into mystic and sacred forms, as of the laws heavenly and eternal, whose "seat is the bosom of God."*

When Crito urges his beloved master to escape from the death that had been unjustly decreed for him, Socrates replies in a noble personification of the Laws, as rebuking him for the thought of such an attempt to evade them; and he must be dim-sighted, indeed, who does not see in the forms of the State Laws, the shadows of the Eternal Laws, august and awful, whose constraint was round about his will. That is the vision which we catch through every form of law, sanitary, social, or ecclesiastical, in the Bible. In the earliest code of the Hebrew statutes known to us, a collection of tribal "Judgments" or "dooms," this high and mystic sense of obligation steals over us. Amid the quaint enactments recorded in the Book of Covenants, whose language carries us back to times of extreme simplicity, we hear the words

Ye shall be holy men unto me.*

Our new critics may tell you that the late poet, who wrote that long-drawn sigh of desire for the Law which is bodied in the One hundred and nine-

---

* Exodus, xx. 31.

teenth Psalm, was thinking of the "Thorah"—the ritual law of the temple and the counsels of the priests. They are doubtless right, if so be that they do not lead you to infer that this devout soul was thinking *only* of the ecclesiastical law. Through it, there was rising upon his spirit the vision of the Law Eternal and Heavenly, the norm and pattern of the law that on earth binds men to purity and righteousness.

> Blessed are those that are undefiled in the way,
> Who walk in the law of the Lord.
> Make me to understand the way of thy commandments;
> And so shall I talk of thy wondrous works.
> Thy statutes have been my songs
> In the house of my pilgrimage.
> The earth, O Lord, is full of thy mercy:
> O teach me thy statutes!
> Thy hands have made me and fashioned me:
> O give me understanding, that I may learn thy commandments.
> Forever, O Lord, thy word is settled in heaven.
> They continue this day, according to thy ordinances.
> Thy righteousness is an everlasting righteousness,
> And thy law is the truth.
> Shew the light of thy countenance upon thy servant,
> And teach me thy statutes.

This is none other than that law of which a far later ecclesiastic, writing also of ecclesiastical law, discoursed in this wise:

> There can be no less acknowledged than that her seat is the bosom of God, her voice the harmony of the world; all things in heaven and earth do her homage, the very least as feeling her care, and the greatest as not exempted from her power: both

angels and men and creatures of what condition soever, though each in different sort and manner, yet all, with uniform consent, admiring her as the mother of their peace and joy.*

This law is none other than that holy form which a modern poet thus apostrophizes:

> Stern lawgiver! yet thou dost wear
> The godhead's most benignant grace;
> Nor know we anything so fair
> As is the smile upon thy face.
> Flowers laugh before thee on their beds,
> And fragrance in thy footing treads;
> Thou dost preserve the stars from wrong;
> And the most ancient heavens, through thee, are fresh and strong.

3. *The Law thus mystic and sacred is seen to be both the law of nature and the law of the human soul.*

The Bible recognizes no duality of natural law and revealed law. All divine law is natural, and, as such, is a revelation. Physical and moral laws are but different forms of one and the same order. The same Power is working in the world around man and in the world within man. The lower forms of Its action are to be interpreted by Its higher forms. Nature is to be resolved by Man. The Ten Words were given as the statutes of Jehovah, himself the personification of some form of nature's force. Out of this simple germ grew the

---

* Richard Hooker: Laws of Ecclesiastical Polity, Book I., ch. xvi. § 8.

ETHICAL AND SPIRITUAL USE OF THE BIBLE.   241

noble thought which anticipated the knowledge of our *savans* and the intuitions of our seers; who unite in showing us one order in the starry heavens and in the mysteries of mind. Thus it is that the Bible feeds so richly, when read aright, that awe which steals upon us as we face nature and see ourselves mirrored there in shadowy outline; and realize the One in all things—God.

There is a beautiful illustration of this in a noble poem that our later critics have handled with a strange lack of perceptiveness. The Nineteenth Psalm opens with a lofty apostrophe to Nature, commencing:

> The heavens declare the glory of God,
> And the firmament sheweth His handywork.

At the seventh verse the Psalm abruptly passes to a eulogy of "The Law"—the moral law shrined in the priestly Thorah:

> The law of the Lord is an undefiled law,
> Converting the soul;
> The testimony of the Lord is sure,
> And giveth wisdom unto the simple.

Here we have, say our learned critics, two psalms welded into one, a song of nature and a song of the soul. As though nature and man did not form one divine poem in two cantos! As though the system of the world around us did not type the world within us! As though it were not always the most instinctive action to pass from the sense of an Order in the starry heavens, and the awe thus awakened, to the sense of an Order in the soul of man, and the deeper awe thus roused!

We know that the Hindus and Egyptians made use, each, of one word to express the law of nature and the law of conscience. The physical order interpreted the sense of a moral order.

> The Egyptian *maat*, derived like the Sanskrit *rita*, from merely sensuous impressions, became the name for moral order and righteousness.*

The Nineteenth Psalm is only the expression among the Hebrews of this wide-spread instinct; an instinct which learned critics may lack, but which the poet still inherits; as the Sphynx whispers to him of the double life of nature and of man, that yet are

<blockquote>
By one music enchanted,
One Deity stirred.
</blockquote>

4. *The Bible leads us on to that sense of sin, in the presence of this " Law," which no lower thought of law can quicken.*

Violations of physiological law Nature stamps as folly. Offences against social laws the State brands as crime. Transgressions of Ideal and Eternal Law become sin. It is not only fool-

---

* Le Page Renouf: Hibbert Lectures, 1879, p. 250.

ish or disgraceful to break the moral law, it is wrong. This is the sense of guilt in disobedience that is roused in each of us by the Bible, as by no other book; that has been quickened in Europe, historically, by these sacred Scriptures, as by no other writings. The Bible has given to humanity a new and intense ethical perception of evil.

The strenuous moral earnestness of the Puritan and the Methodist is vitalized from these books. The very type of saintship in Christendom is unique. It is no mere ceremonial correctness for which the priestly Ezekiel pleads with tender pathos:

Repent, and turn yourselves from all your transgressions whereby ye have transgressed, and make you a clean heart and a new spirit; for why will ye die, O house of Israel?

It is this intense sense of the exceeding sinfulness of sin which oppressed the great-hearted Paul, and wrung from him the bitter cry:

O wretched man that I am! Who shall deliver me from the body of this death.

How vividly this sense of sin expresses itself in the Fifty-first Psalm! There is here a plaint infinitely deeper than the chagrin and remorse of the man who has committed an "indiscretion," or become entangled in an "intrigue;" there is the cry of a soul that has betrayed its highest, holiest fidelities, and lies low in the dust before the Heavenly purity:

> Wash me throughly from my wickedness,
> And cleanse me from my sin.
> Cast me not away from Thy presence,
> And take not Thy Holy Spirit from me.

To enter into the spirit of this sigh of penitence is a new knowledge of the human heart. The Bible thus leads men to live as in the presence of an awful Power of Holiness, which is searching through and through our beings. We cannot understand the Biblical "salvation" unless we have fathomed, at least, the shoaler experiences of these saintly souls of old, and know some little of the depths of sin.

5. *The Bible wakens in the breast of man an ethical passion for the ideal and eternal law, which, apart from early Buddhism, has no parallel in history.*

The prophets are aflame with the ardors of this sacred enthusiasm. The ordinary passions of mankind are rivaled in intensity by the mystic passion of their souls for the Heavenly Wisdom. They stand amid the wild whirl of selfish strife in the society of their day, and lift on high the holy forms of Justice and Brotherhood, as though expecting their commonplace cotemporaries to turn aside from practical affairs, and seek for them; and, so subtle and searching are the appeals of these heavenly visions, men do actually turn from mammon to worship these impoverishing divinities; and a great movement arises, looking to the bringing down of these ideals upon the earth, as the ruling powers in the court and the exchange. The regenerating force of Christendom has lain in the coming of these prophets, generation after generation, to the children of men, to lead them upon the mount where they should clearly see those lofty shapes, commanding instant loyalty from honest souls. The ominous travail-throes of society to-day await one stimulus to free the new order that is struggling to the birth—the passion for ethical and social ideals, which the Bible, rightly administered, would inspire.

The prophetic spirit is the vital force of the Bible. Its insistent power reappears in Paul; a man consuming in the fires of this holy passion, and kindling its ardors in the souls of untold myriads. His great letter to the Romans, so strangely misread as a mere dogmatic treatise, breathes and burns with this lofty enthusiasm. Its central thought, its threading *motif*, heard anew in every critical movement of the argument, is—Righteousness. The Master in whom the Bible centres, enriches earth with a new benediction:

> Blessed are they which do hunger and thirst after righteousness.

This highest passion of mankind is wakened by the Bible as by no other book. Through it, the mystic Forerunners reveal themselves to the human soul most alluringly; enthralling it with their pure charms, dispelling the illusions of the senses and the glamor of the world, in the light of their holy loveliness. The Eternal Wisdom calls from out these pages to the sons of men:

<blockquote>Hearken unto me ye that follow after righteousness.</blockquote>

6. *The Bible reveals these ethical ideals as no mere alluring visions, but as the substantial realities of being.*

Men say to those who speak of these high conceptions—"They are the dreams of sentimentalists, the will-'o-the-wisp lights that beguile men away from the *terra firma;* to be trusted and followed by no practical man." "Idealist" is a term of reproach. And justly, from any other point of view than that which the Bible, true to the most penetrating discernment of humanity, opens to us. These ideal forms are not the empty conceits of man's brain, bred from the fumes of his boundless egotism. They are not the clouds that gather and form and break into airy unreality in the atmosphere of earth. They are the shadows falling upon the soul of man from the unseen Realities, which alone have substantial and abiding being. The laws of nature are surely not the baseless fabric of a dream. These ideals are simply those laws, transfigured into their spiritual substances. Whatever in our blindness we may persuade ourselves elsewhere, over the Bible we recognize the true character of the visions which so strangely stir us. This is the power of the Bible. Christian seemed to Mr. Worldly Wiseman a fool. But he saw the heavenly city, and trudged along, sure that time would prove him in the right. Christian carried in his hand this Book. With this Book in our hands, we, too, are sure that the visions of Purity and Justice, which we dimly see afar, are substantial and real, and that man will win at the last to the land where they are the light thereof.

Whereupon I was not disobedient to the heavenly vision.

7. *The Bible thus inspires a buoyancy and exhilaration which feed the fresh forces of all noble life.*

No poet is needed to tell us that

Virtue kindles at the touch of joy.

We know it in our own experience. We notice it in every great revival of religion. We trace it through the history of Christianity. The story of the early days of Jesus is, as Renan called it, "a delightful pastoral." In the person of humanity's greatest idealist, the highest joy of the soul was set in the framing of one of nature's brightest scenes. Even from the shadows of the garden of Gethsemane, He bequeaths to his little flock the legacy of his free spirit: My joy I leave with you. The Christian Society entered into that be-quest, and in its first exhilaration overflowed the hard coast lines of property, and realized a happy brotherhood.

> And all that believed were together, and had all things common; and sold their possessions and goods and parted them to all men as any man had need. And they, continuing daily with one accord in the temple, and breaking bread at home did take their food with gladness.

The prophets were filled with a buoyancy of spirit that scarce would let them keep down to the plodding steps of social progress; that constantly rapt them away into the future, whence their voices echo back the gladness of their visions. The good time is coming on the earth. The longings of man's soul are to be realized. Crushed by no disappointments, wearied out by no delays, the prophets maintain an indomitable hopefulness; their voices the carollings of the birds that greet the dawn of day:

> Sing, O Heavens; and be joyful, O earth;
> And break forth into singing, O mountains.
> For the Lord hath comforted his people;
> And will have mercy upon his afflicted.

One treads here the upper zones, where the air is rare and every draught an inspiration; where the Laws are seen majestically sweeping every force into the measured movement which is making all things work together for good to them that love God.

With a tact truer than any theory, our canon of scripture has been closed in the Book of the Revelation; whose visions look beyond the break-up of Jerusalem and shadow on the far horizon, where earth and heaven melt in one, the fair form of the City of God, coming down from out the skies upon the new world wherein dwelleth righteousness.

In these days, when "joy is withered from the sons of men," it is like drinking from the Castalian springs to draw within our souls from the Bible the sense of that kingdom of God which is joy in the Holy Ghost; into which men are to come

>With everlasting joy upon their heads:
>They shall obtain joy and gladness
>And sorrow and sighing shall flee away.

You learn the power of the Bible as you find how the joy of the Lord is your strength.

8. *The Bible leads this sense of Law into that awful vision wherein " Conscious Law is King of kings."*

The Laws appear substantial and real inasmuch as they are seen to be but phases of the Infinite and Eternal Being, the Righteous Lord who loveth righteousness. It is a conscious, intelligent, holy Being, whom Israel worships through these ideal forms of goodness. However He transcended their poor personalities, as transcend them they knew He must, God was yet best expressed in the form of the human, conscious personality. Man, the highest creature, must be, they said, most nearly in the form of God. As man takes up the noblest characteristics of the life below him, so his own noblest characteristics must be taken up into the Lord of Life. God cannot be less than personal, however much more than personal He may be. He is to be thought of by us, in lack of nobler imagination, as personal. Israel thus grew into the conception of the Infinite Power, manifest in the order of nature and in the order of conscience, as conscious Power; One in whose image man was made, the Father of the mystic "I"; whose nature is the law of creation, whose purpose is its plan, whose will is its exhaustless energy.

This is the secret which has kept the religions inspired by the Bible from lapsing, as other religions have done, into lifelessness.

Egypt was the land of a religion which had won a high conception of the Divine unity; a religion which was scientific in its forms of thought, and earnestly moral in its spirit; but which failed to keep distinct in mind the order of nature from the Being on whom it reposes, and thus sank into the dreamy pantheism of its cultured classes, and the poetic polytheisms of its people. Of this lapse, Renouf writes:

> All gods were in fact but names of the One who resided in them all. But this God is no other than Nature. Both indi-

viduals and entire nations may long continue to hold this view, without drawing the inevitable conclusion, that if there is no other God than this, the world is really without a God. But the fate of a religion which involves such a conclusion, and with that conclusion the loss of faith in immortality, and even in the distinction of Right and Wrong, except so far as they are connected with ritual prescriptions, is inevitably sealed.*

Neither Judaism, nor Mohammedanism, nor Christianity, the religions fed directly or indirectly from the Bible, have run, or can well run into this fatal error. The Divine Being who is mirrored in the Bible is the Conscious Intelligence to whom alone of right belongs that ineffable name—GOD. This is the thought and this is the word which hold the spell of the Bible power over the human soul. Nowhere else is the sense of God so alive, nowhere else does it so thrill the whole being of man. It was this living God whom these holy men of old were seeking; not simply the august ideals of the soul, but the Eternal Being who casts them as his shadows upon man:

> Unto Thee lift I up mine eyes,
> O Thou that dwellest in the heavens.
>
> . . . . . .
>
> My soul truly waiteth still upon God,
> For of Him cometh my salvation.
>
> . . . . . .
>
> Like as the hart desireth the water-brooks,
> So longeth my soul after Thee, O God.

---

* Hibbert Lectures, 1879, p. 279.

> My soul is athirst for God, yea, even for the Living God;
> When shall I come to appear before the presence of God?

It is God whom these holy men find. The Ineffable Presence rejoices their souls, and as we keep company with them rejoices our souls also:

> Lord, Thou hast been our home
> From one generation to another.
> . . . . . .
> Whoso dwelleth in the secret-place of the Most High
> Shall abide under the shadow of the Almighty.
> . . . . . .
> O Lord, Thou hast searched me out and known me.
> Thou knowest my down-sitting and mine up-rising;
> Thou understandest my thoughts afar off.
> Thou art about my path and about my bed,
> And spiest out all my ways.
> For lo, there is not a word in my tongue
> But Thou, O Lord, knowest it altogether.

The inspirations which we feel from the Bible-words are the breathings of the Eternal Spirit. The Divine whispers, which are too often inarticulate in nature and even in our souls, are articulate in the great Bible-words—the words proceeding from out of the mouth of God, on which man iveth. The power of the Bible is that the deafest souls can therein hear—GOD.

9. *God speaks in* A MAN.

The Bible centres in the story of a life which was so filled with the Holy Ghost that this Man became the symbol of the Most High, the sacrament of His Being and Presence, the sacred shrine of Deity. As when the long-drawn travail of instrumentation labors through the opening movements of the ninth symphony, with a strain too fine for any voicing save by man, there bursts at length upon the tumultuous storm of sound the clear, high, song of joy from human lips; so from the mounting efforts of a nation's insufficient utterance there rises at last a voice, which takes up every groaning of the Spirit in humanity into the perfect beauty of a human life divine.

> And so the Word hath breath, and wrought
> With human hands the creed of creeds,
> In loveliness of perfect deeds,
> More strong than all poetic thought.

The light of the Son of Man is the life of men; the light for our minds and the warmth for our hearts. In the Power in whom we live and move and have our being, we see "Our Father who art in Heaven." In the laws of life we read the methods of His schooling of our souls. In the sorrows of life we receive His disciplinings. In the sins that cling so hard upon us we feel the evils of our imperfection, from which He is seeking to deliver us through His training of our spirits. In the shame of sin we are conscious of the guilt that His free forgiveness wipes away, when we turn saying, Father, I have sinned. In death we face the door-way to some other room of the Father's house, where, it may be, just beyond the threshold our dear ones wait for us! In Christ himself we own our heaven-sent Teacher, Master, Saviour, Friend; our elder Brother, who in our sinful flesh lives our holy aspirations, and, smiling, beckons us to follow Him, whispering in our ears—To them that receive me I give " power to become the sons of God."

The power of the Bible is—CHRIST.

II.

When Sir Walter Scott lay in his last illness, he asked Lockhart one day to read to him. "From what book shall I read?" said Lockhart. "There is but one book," was Scott's answer. Those who have sought the "power to become the sons of God" will understand this hyperbole of the most healthy human mind in modern English literature. Tested by experience there is indeed, in the wide range of the literature of power, no book to be mentioned with the Bible for feeding the life of God in man. Our fathers found this true, and their children cannot correct their judgment. The substitute for the Bible, as an ethical and spiritual instructor, is not out.

I speak to those who are in earnest in the building of a man. You need this book, my brothers. Luther's higher life dated from his discovery of the Bible. Have you discovered the Bible? Within the body of human "letters" have you found out the divine soul of the Bible? Through the chorus of human voices have you heard the voice of the Eternal Power? If not, life holds one more rich "find" for you—a treasure hidden in the field over which you have so lightly strayed.

Buy a Bible, my brothers! The current coin of the land, in the shops of our best booksellers, may have failed to buy for you a real Bible. No noble book is ever to be made your own in this easy fashion. Ruskin tells us that the great picture will not give itself to us unless we give ourselves to it. The Bible must have its price. The best comes dearest. If you will not pay you cannot buy. Pay for the real Bible your costliest offering of mind and heart. Spend upon it, day by day, your careful, reverent study, until beneath your love the Book warms into life; and, having proven well your loyalty, this teacher of the soul opens its soul to you and whispers— Henceforth I call you not servant but friend. Wait in these courts until the Eternal Wisdom, who walks within this temple, turns her face upon you, "mystic, wonderful;" and the common places grow refulgent with a new and heavenly beauty, and you humbly say—This is none other but the house of God, and this is the gate of heaven.

How shall we thus rightly read the Bible, for

ethical and spiritual upbuilding? Let me offer some plain and practical suggestions to this end.

(1.) *Read it daily.*

Your soul needs its daily bread. Do not starve your soul. Do not try to fatten it on chaff. Get the best soul-food, the long tried manna that forms upon these pages day by day, for him who will be at pains to gather it. He must be busy, indeed, who cannot find time to keep himself alive.

(2.) *Read it in the choicest moments of the day.*

The best picture should have the best setting. Our fathers' symbol of the opening of a new day was the opening of the Bible. Their symbol of the closing of another day's duties was the closing of the Bible. Can we improve upon their ritual? John Quincy Adams noted in his journal his custom of reading in the Bible each morning, of which he well observed:

It seems to me the most suitable manner of beginning the day.

Pitch the day aright with this tuning-fork, and hush the babel-voices of the world to its tones of peace at night.

(3.) *Read the Bible whenever you need some special influence of strength or cheer, amid the temptations and trials of the day.*

It holds the unfailing corrective for the manifold disorders of our busy lives. To think its thoughts and breathe its desires, even for a few moments, is to have the horizon of the senses open, the heavy atmosphere of earth clear, the illusions of the world evanish, the fever of business cool and calm, the tempting appetites and passions slink down shamed into their kennels. It is to have the dark look of life lighten, the sting of disappointment lose its venom, the weariness of sickness forget itself, and the sorrow of the stricken heart sob itself asleep within the everlasting arms of One who, like a mother, comforteth his children, and who with his own hand wipes away the tears from our eyes.

A few days after one of the battles before Richmond, a Southern soldier was found unburied. His right hand still clasped a Bible, and his stiff fingers pressed upon the words of the Twenty-third Psalm:

> I will fear no evil, for Thou art with me;
> Thy rod and Thy staff they comfort me.

(4.) *In the choice of these daily readings, follow the guidance of the soul's sure instinct.*

You need no critical knowledge to teach you what parts of the Bible are the most highly inspired. The spiritual sense will appraise these books aright. As the beasts are led instinctively to the herbs that hold healing for their ailments, so you shall find the tonic and the balm that you need. You will naturally pasture for the most part in the Prophets, the Psalms, the Gospels, the great Epistles of Paul, the First Epistle of John, and kindred writings. You may dip into these books as the bees dip into the flowers, now burying themselves in the luscious honeysuckle, and now lingering on the rich rose, if so be that you only suck sweetness into your soul.

(5.) *Wheresoever you read, read in the spirit.*

"I was in the spirit on the Lord's day," wrote the seer. If he had been in the understanding merely, he would not have had many visions. The Spirit must interpret the Spirit's words. The Bible requires, as Bushnell wrote :

Divine inbreathings and exaltations in us, that we may asscend into their meanings.*

In his last sickness Archbishop Usher was observed, one day, sitting in his wheel-chair, with a Bible in his lap, and moving his position as the sun stole round to the westward, so as to let the light fall on the sacred page. That is a symbol of the right use of the Bible.

I picked up lately the choice Bible which I selected for myself as a boy, and on the fly-leaf, in my boyish hand, I read the words:

Open Thou mine eyes that I may behold wondrous things out of Thy law.

---

* God in Christ, p. 93.

I still find that the best commentator, for the ethical and spiritual use of the Bible, is one Master Praying Always.

As the bard with the Muse, so the critic in the presence of Wisdom, must forget his skill; "must be, with good intent, no more his, but hers:"

> Must throw away his pen and paint,
>   Kneel with worshipers.
>
> Then, perchance, a sunny ray,
>   From the heaven of fire,
> His lost tools may overpay,
>   And better his desire.

Thus buying Bibles for yourselves, my friends, see that your children buy themselves the Bible in the same good coin.

(a.) *Read with them the tales of its noble men.*

Do not hesitate to read with them these stories of the ancients, because there may be the commingling of legend with history, of myth with fact. You do not hesitate to read them the story of William Tell, although there are woven into it the elements of a very old and wide-spread sun-myth. These mythic elements have been woven around some real historic hero, and the spirit of his heroism breathes through every fold of the drapery. How charmingly Kingsley tells the tales of the Grecian heroes! Through his crystalline language we seem to inhale the crisp, clear air of the morning of Greece, in which the simple souls of child-men thus shaped their dreams of duty around their older dreams of nature. Conscience fashioned these primitive fancies upon its form, and pulses through them its quickening life; the touch of which makes our children buoyant with aspiration, so that they mount on high, like Perseus of the winged feet.

Thus read the matchless stories of the Hebrews, mindless of legend or of myth. The Spirit of Holiness breathing through these tales will inspire the souls of the children, without restraint from the questions that the reason may raise. Tell them no lies if they ask you questions. Read these ancient stories *as* stories, of good and noble men; stories written down long ago, and told from father to son through longer ages before they were thus written out. Leave the children to detect the legendary elements. I find them quick enough at that work without parental help. The bright child feels the unreal in the tales that he most loves; but he loves them none the less, perhaps all the more, because of the spell upon his imagination that he would not break; while through them, upon his open soul, streams in the holy power of these sacred stories. Do you concern yourselves with impressing the moral of these God-breathed tales.

Read with your children the stories of the dear Master, and make His life grow real to them, till

He shall draw them after **Him**, in the steps of **His** most holy life.

(b.) *Form in the children the habit of daily reading in the Bible.*

Say to each of them, in your own way, that which Sir Matthew Hale wrote to his child :

> Every morning read seriously and reverently a portion of the Holy Scriptures. It is a book full of light and wisdom, and will make you wise to eternal life.

(c.) *Cultivate in them a genuine interest in the Bible.*

The aids to an intelligent interest in the Bible-books are now so plentiful, and the human charm of them is so great, that it ought to be an easy thing for a parent to awaken a real fondness for these immortal writings. The best safeguard against bad taste in literature or life is the formation of a good taste. These are books, to learn to love which is the making of a man. Our children may not grow into the genius, but they will grow into somewhat of the goodness of the illustrious and saintly John Henry Newman, if, in after years, they can write the first lines of their autobiographies in the words which open the biographical part of the *Apologia Pro Vita Sua:*

> I was brought up from a child to take great delight in reading the Bible.

(d.) *Train the children to commit to memory the choicest passages of the Bible.*

John Ruskin doubtless, at the time, rebelled against the strict rule of his good aunt, which kept him busy on the Sundays memorizing the Scriptures; but he is thankful now, as he has owned, for the discipline which stored his mind with their creative words. What a treasury of holy thoughts and influences does he carry within him who has written on his mind such passages as the nineteenth, twenty-third, ninety-first, one hundred and third, and one hundred and thirty-ninth Psalms; the third and eighth chapters of Proverbs; the fortieth chapter of Isaiah; the sermon on the mount, the parable of the prodigal son, and the thirteenth chapter of first Corinthians. Happy he who, like the palm tree in the desert, can strike his roots below the arid surface of the world into fresh and living waters, and thus keep life green amid the droughts of earth. The parable of the temptation of Christ should teach us how to arm our children against the wiles of the Evil One, whom they must surely meet: "And he said, It is written." In the stress and strain of conflict, when the air is dimmed with the dust of the contending forces and the vision grows confused, it is a saving sound to hear the ringing call of Duty, from the hills where One watcheth over the battle-field. When sore pressed by the foe, it may prove our victory to fall back against the strong stone wall of an external authority, that can hold our lines unbroken. It is no wonder that the tempting sailors could do nothing with the cabin-boy who was "chock full of the Bible."

(e.) *Teach your children, as you teach yourselves, to hearken through these voices of the human writers to the voice of God.*

Bother then with no theories of inspiration. Never deny nor conceal the true human voices of these men who spake of old, but never fail to affirm the true Divine breath in these men who spake as they were moved by the Holy Ghost. And, since this is the power of the Bible, emphasize the Divine speaking; make every God-breathed word sound to the children's souls as the very voice of God; until, in simple faith and reverent docility, they shall each answer—Speak, Lord : Thy servant heareth!

> Thy word is a lamp unto my feet,
> And a light unto my path.

Such is the holy office of the Bible : such be its blessed service to our souls, and to the souls of our dear children! May we walk in its light through life; that in the valley of the shadow of death that light may still fall upon us.

It is not many months since I was called to the

house where, in a ripe and honored age, lay a warden of this church, stricken suddenly by death. On the table in his room, as he had left it open after reading in it that morning, I saw a Bible.

I can ask for my funeral no better symbol of the aim and effort of my poor erring life, if so be it shame me not too much, than that which told the story of an humble servant of the Lord. Upon his coffin, with the book-mark between the pages where he last had read, was—his Bible!

Blessed Lord, who hast caused all holy Scriptures to be written for our learning; grant that we may in such wise hear them, read, mark, learn, and inwardly digest them, that by patience and comfort of Thy Holy Word, we may embrace and ever hold fast the blessed hope of everlasting life, which Thou has given us in our Saviour, Jesus Christ. *Amen.*

THE END.

ENOCH MORGAN'S SONS.
SAPOLIO
FOR CLEANING AND POLISHING

The Cheapest and Best
Scouring Soap,
IN THE WORLD.
Price 10c. per Cake.

JUST PUBLISHED:

PROGRESS AND POVERTY,
By HENRY GEORGE.

1 Vol., 16mo, Lovell's Library No. 52, ...20

If we were asked to name the most important work of the Nineteenth Century, we would name "Progress and Poverty."—*New York Era.*

A new edition of Canon Farrar's great work,

EARLY DAYS OF CHRISTIANITY,

1 Vol., 12mo, cloth, gilt, - - - - - - - - - - $1.00
1 " " half calf. - - - - - - - - - 2.50

This edition is printed from large, clear type, on good paper and very attractively bound. The half-calf edition will make a very handsome Christmas present for your Clergyman or Sunday School Teacher. The above work is also issued in 2 vols., in neat paper covers, as No. 50, Lovell's Library.
No. 50. Early Days of Christianity, by Canon Farrar, - Part I, .20
" " " " " " " " " II, .20

Recently Published:

Divorce, an original Novel, by Margaret Lee. 1 Vol. 12mo, neat paper cover, - - - - - - - - - - - .20
1 Vol., 12mo cloth, black and gold, - - - - - - .50

A powerful American Novel, dealing with a subject of vital importance at the present day.

JOHN W. LOVELL CO., Publishers,
14 AND 16 VESEY STREET, NEW YORK.

STANDARD PUBLICATIONS.

Chas. Dickens' Complete Works, 15 Vols., 12mo, cloth, gilt, $22.50.
W. M. Thackeray's Complete Works, 11 Vols., 12mo, cloth, gilt, $16.50.

George Eliot's Complete Works, 8 Vols., 12mo, cloth, gilt, $10.00.
Plutarch's Lives of Illustrious Men, 3 Vols., 12mo. cloth, gilt, $4.50.

JOHN W. LOVELL CO., Publishers,
14 AND 16 VESEY STREET, NEW YORK.

STANDARD PUBLICATIONS.

Rollins' Ancient History, 4 Vols., 12mo, cloth, gilt, $6.00.
Charles Knight's Popular History of England, 8 Vols., 12mo, cloth, gilt top, $12.00.

Lovell's Series of Red Line Poets, 50 Volumes of all the best works of the world's great Poets, Tennyson, Shakespere, Milton, Meredith, Ingelow, Proctor, Scott, Byron, Dante, &c. $1.25 per volume.

JOHN W. LOVELL CO., Publishers,
14 AND 16 VESEY STREET, NEW YORK.

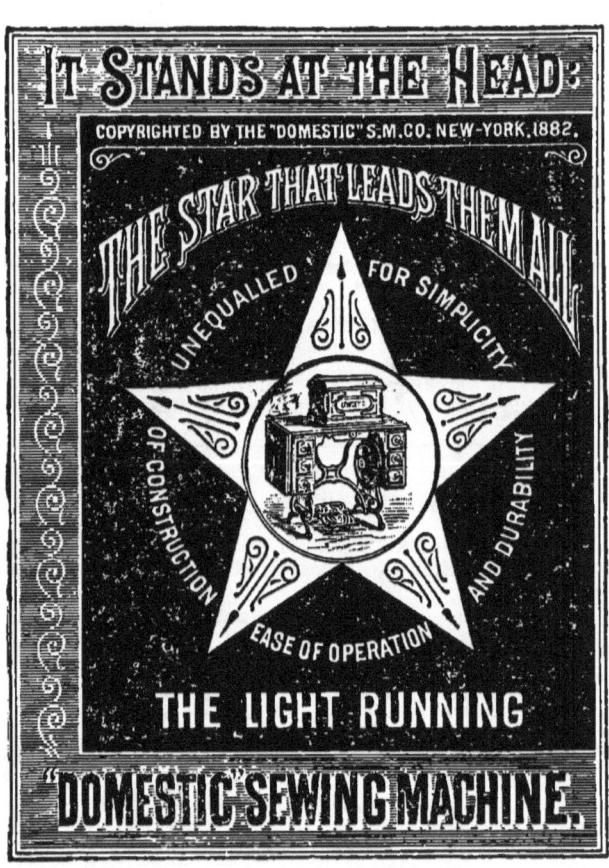

[*January*, 1883.

JOHN W. LOVELL COMPANY'S
DESCRIPTIVE CATALOGUE OF
Standard *and* Miscellaneous Books.

Alexander (Mrs.) Works by
The Wooing O't. By MRS. ALEXANDER. 1 vol., 16mo. Cloth extra, black and gold...50 cts.
Also in paper covers, in Lovell's Library, in two parts, each............15 cts.

The Admiral's Ward. By MRS. ALEXANDER. 1 vol., 16mo, cloth extra, black and gold..50 cts.
Also in paper covers, in Lovell's Library. *In press*...............20 cts

American Illustrated Pronouncing Dictionary of the English Language. Containing upwards of 25,000 words, Orthography, Pronunciation and Definitions, according to the best English and American Lexicographers. With an Appendix containing Abbreviations, Foreign Words and Phrases, etc. Illustrated with over 200 engravings, strongly bound in cloth.....................30 cts.

Andersen, (Hans Christian).
Fairy Tales. By HANS CHRISTIAN ANDERSEN. New plates, large clear type, handsomely printed and illustrated. 1 vol., 12mo, cloth, black and gold..$1 00

Anstey, (F.)
Vice-Versa, or, a Lesson to Fathers. By F. ANSTEY. 1 vol., 16mo, cloth extra, black and gold...50 cts.
Also in paper covers, Lovell's Library No. 30..........................20 cts.

Arabian Nights Entertainment.
The Thousand and One Nights. Translated from the Arabic. New plates, large clear type. 1 vol., 12mo., illustrated, cloth, black and gold...$1 00

Generations of wise fathers and mothers have thoroughly proved the high educational value of the ARABIAN NIGHTS *as a book of amusing stories for children. They stimulate young minds and create a taste and desire for reading at a time when almost all other forms of literature would be irksome and uninstructive. Hardly any one that does not date the first real impulse given to his intellectual faculties back to his first acquaintance with* SINBAD THE SAILOR, ALADDIN AND HIS WONDERFUL LAMP, *and the* HISTORY OF THE ENCHANTED HORSE. *Beside the infinite enjoyment that is afforded the child, a familiarity with the characteristic features of Oriental literature is acquired which is of permanent value in the education of after years.*

Aytoun (William Edmondstone).
Lays of the Scottish Cavaliers and other Poems. By WILLIAM EDMONDSTONE AYTOUN, Professor of Rhetoric and English Literature in the University of Edinburgh. Red Line Edition. 1 vol., 12mo. Cloth, gilt, gilt edges. $1 25.

Professor Aytoun has selected his themes from striking incidents and stirring scenes in mediæval Scotch history, and thrown over them the light of an imagination at once picturesque and powerful. Finer ballads than these are not to be found in the English language, if in any. Full of the true fire, they now stir and swell with the stirring ring of the trumpet, now sink in cadences sad and wild as a Highland dirge. We feel, when we read these lays, that we are dealing not with shadows, but with living men. The poems which form part of the volume with the Lays are gems which, while they add to the poet's reputation for versatility, add also to his fame; what they lack of the heroic element which makes the ballads so fascinating, they make up in a charm wholly their author's and their own.

Besant (Walter) and James Rice.
They Were Married. By WALTER BESANT and JAMES RICE. 16mo, paper covers, Lovell's Library No. 18...................10 cts.

Björnson (Björnstjerne).
The Happy Boy and Arne. Tales of Norwegian Country Life. Two vols. in one. 16mo, cloth extra, black and gold.......50 cts.
Also, published separately in Lovell's Library—
No. 3. The Happy Boy. Paper cover...............................10 cts.
No. 4. Arne. Paper covers...10 cts.

Balzac (Honoré de).
The Vendetta; tales of Love and Passion. By HONORÉ DE BALZAC. 1 vol., 16mo, cloth, black and gold......................50 cts.
Also, in paper covers, in Lovell's Library.........................20 cts.

Black (William).
A Princess of Thule. By WM. BLACK. 1 vol., 16mo, cloth extra, black and gold..50 cts.
Also, in paper covers, Lovell's Library No. 48.....................20 cts.
An Adventure in Thule and Marriage of Moira Fergus. By WM. BLACK. Paper covers, Lovell's Library No. 40............10 cts.

Broughton (Rhoda).

Second Thoughts. By RHODA BROUGHTON, 1 vol., 16mo, cloth, black and gold...50 cts.
Also, in paper covers, Lovell's Library No. 23....................20 cts.

Bulwer's Novels.

One-volume Edition. Containing a selection of the best novels of Sir EDWARD BULWER (Lord Lytton), as follows:—

The Last Days of Pompeii.	Eugene Aram.
Ernest Maltravers.	Pelham.
Alice.	Zanoni.
Godolphin.	

1 vol., 8vo., cloth, black and gold..................................$2 00
Also see LYTTON, LORD.

Bunyan (John).

The Pilgrim's Progress from this World to that which is to come, delivered under the similitude of a dream. By JOHN BUNYAN. 1 vol., 12mo, illustrated, cloth, black and gold..................$1 00

Burns (Robert).

The complete Poetical Works of ROBERT BURNS, to which is added his correspondence. Large, clear type, new plates. Red Line Edition. 1 vol., 12mo, handsomely bound in cloth, gilt, gilt edges..$1 25

Burns is by far the greatest poet that ever sprung from the bosom of the people. He was born a poet, if ever man was, and his rank, as Byron said, " is the first in his art." He possessed all the essentials of a poet's great humor, great powers of description, great discrimination of character, and great pathos. His conceptions are all original, his thoughts new, and his style unborrowed. His language is familiar, yet dignified, careless, yet concise; he sheds a redeeming light on all he touches, and whatever he glances at rises into life and beauty. His variety is equal to his originality. It is as infinite as his power in expression, and the result of these combined faculties has been such verse as the world will, in all liklihood, never see again. Long after more pretentious rhyme writers have been forgotten, the poet of the fields and of the cotter's cabin will be quoted wherever the language he became illustrious in is known.

Byron, Lord.

The complete Poetical Works of LORD BYRON, printed in clear type on good paper. Red Line Edition. 1 vol., 12mo, illustrated, cloth gilt, gilt edges...$1 25

" In the United States, Byron will always occupy a high place as the poet of the passions, and it is said, that after Shakespeare he is the most popular of the English poets. The least successful of Byron's productions, notwithstanding the admirable passages with which they abound, are his tragedies; the work that gives us the highest notion of his genius, power and versatility is his DON JUAN. *The Don is at times free and almost obscene, and the whole tendency of the poem may be considered immoral; but there are scattered throughout it the most exquisite pieces of writing and feeling—inimitable blendings of wit, humor, raillery and pathos, and by far the finest verses Byron ever wrote. He may be said to have created this manner; for the Bernesco style of the Italians, to which it has been compared, is not like it."—Life and Literary Labors of* LORD BYRON.

Californians and Mormons.
Sketches of American Life, Manners and Institutions. By A. F. D. DE RUPERT. 1 vol., 12mo, cloth, black and gold.........$1 00

Campbell (Thomas).
The Poetical Works of THOMAS CAMPBELL, with Notes and Biographical Sketch. Printed in clear type, on good paper. Red Line Edition. 1 vol., 12mo, illustrated, cloth, gilt, gilt edges......................$1 25

I do not think I overrate the merits of the "Pleasures of Hope," whether taking it in its parts, or as a whole, in preferring it to any didactic poem in the English language. No poet at such an age ever produced such an exquisite specimen of poetical mastery; that is, of fine conception and of high art combined. Sentiments tender, energetic, impassioned, eloquent, majestic, are conveyed to the reader in the tones of a music forever varied, sinking or swelling like the harmonies of an Æolian lyre, yet ever delightful; and these are illustrated by pictures from romance, history, or domestic life, replete with power and beauty.—MOIR'S *Lectures on Poetry.*

"Cavendish."
Card Essays, Clay's Decisions and Card-Table-Talk. By "CAVENDISH," 1 vol., 16mo, cloth, gilt..........................75 cts.

The Laws and Principles of Whist, carefully revised, with diagram cards, printed in two colors; to which is added Card Essays, Clay's Decisions and Card-Table Talk, with portrait of "CAVENDISH." 1 vol., 16mo, cloth, black and gold $1 50

Chaucer (Geoffrey).
The Poetical Works of GEOFFREY CHAUCER, with Memoir. Printed in clear type, on good paper. Red Line Edition. 1 vol., 12mo. Illustrated, cloth, gilt, gilt edges.. .... $1 25

Chaucer has well been called the father of English poetry. In elocution and eloquence, in grace and harmony of versification, he surpassed all his predecessors, and for the first time in English literature created verse which was true poetry, not mere doggrel rhyme. His genius was universal, and the themes he exercised it in, consequently, of boundless variety. He painted familiar manners with the touch of a master, which to this day impresses the reader of the pages penned five centuries ago with the haunting idea that the poet's characters are alive and moving in a pageant before him. His humor was as natural and unforced as his pathos was deep, his sentiment pure, and his passion fiery and genuine. It was Coleridge who said of Chaucer, "I take unceasing delight in him. His manly cheerfulness is especially delicious to me in my old age. How exquisitely tender he is, yet how perfectly free from the least touch of sickly melancholy or morbid drooping." The verdict of Coleridge has been the verdict of the whole reading world.

Child's History of England.
Child's History of England. By CHARLES DICKENS. A New Edition for the use of Schools. With numerous illustrations. Printed from large type, illustrated, 1 vol., 12mo. $1 00

Charles Dickens wrote the Child's History of England for his own children, because as he himself says, he could find nothing in the whole line of English histories just suitable for them; at a time when they were beginning to read with interest and profit, but not sufficiently advanced to take up the great standard authors. It was a labor of love, and had been well appreciated by the multitudes of young people who have gained their first knowledge of history from this delightful little volume. It is written in the most pure and simple language, and has for young readers all the picturesque and vivid interest that one of the author's novels possesses for the older ones. All the great characters of English history become as familiar, and produce as permanent impressions, as the heroes of the Arabian Nights and of the other favorite books of childhood. It is not only indispensable in every household where any care at all is bestowed upon the education of children, but is also one of the best brief and compendious histories of England for all classes of readers.

Also see DICKENS (CHARLES).

Children of the Abbey.
A Tale. By REGINA MARIA ROCHE. 1 vol., 12mo, illustrated, cloth, gilt...$1 00

Of all the once popular novels of this once famous novelist, the "Children of the Abbey" alone remains. From the time of its first republication in this country it has retained its place in popular favor. No better example of the novel of our grandfathers could be found, and few more interesting ones are written in these days of the grandchildren.

Coleridge (Samuel Taylor).
The Poetical Works of SAMUEL TAYLOR COLERIDGE. With an introduction and Memoir. Red Line Edition. 1 vol., 12mo, cloth, gilt-edges..$1 25

Of all the illustrious English men of letters, Coleridge, with his spacious intellect, his subtle and comprehensive intelligence, holds rank with the first. As a poet he will live with the language. On his incomparable "Genevieve" he has lavished all the melting graces of poetry and chivalry; in his "Ancient Mariner" he has sailed, and in his "Christabel" flown to the very limits of invention and belief; and in his chant of "Fire, Famine and Slaughter" he has revived the startling strains of the furies, and given us a song worthy the prime agents of perdition.

Collins (Wilkie).
The Moonstone. By WILKIE COLLINS. 1 vol., 16mo, cloth, black and gold ....50 cts.
Also, in two volumes, Nos. 8 and 9, Lovell's Library, each............10 cts.
The New Magdalen. By WILKIE COLLINS. 1 vol., 16mo, cloth, black and gold..50 cts.
Also, in paper covers, Lovell's Library No. 24..........................20 cts.

Cooper (J. Fenimore).
The Last of the Mohicans: A Narrative of 1757. By J. FENIMORE COOPER. Printed from large, clear type. 1 vol., 12mo, cloth, black and gold $1 00
Also in paper covers, Lovell's Library No. 26............................20 cts.
The Spy. By J. FENIMORE COOPER. 16mo, paper covers, Lovell's Library, No. 53...20 cts.

Cowper (William).
The complete Poetical Works of WILLIAM COWPER. Printed from new plates, large, clear type, handsomely illustrated. Red Line Edition. 1 vol., 12mo, cloth, black and gold, gilt edges............$1 25

Cowper was the poet of well educated and well principled England. His muse was as pure as his style, and his life conformed to both. His "Task" is a poem of such infinite variety that it seems to include all possible subjects. It contains pictures of domestic comfort and social refinement which can only be forgotten with the language itself.

Crabbe (George).

The Poetical Works of GEORGE CRABBE. Red Line Edition. 1 vol., 12mo, illustrated, cloth, gilt, gilt edges....................$1 25

Dr. Johnson, to whom Crabbe's first poem, "The Village," was submitted, pronounced it "original, vigorous and elegant." The public endorsed the great lexicographer's opinion, and Crabbe deserved it. His genius was essentially analytic and humane. He had a mortal hatred of wrong, and was never so active as when laying it bare to the world.

Dante Alighieri.

The Vision of Hell, Purgatory, and Paradise, of DANTE ALIGHIERI. Translated by the Rev. Henry Francis Cary, A. M. With the life of Dante and Chronological View of his age. Red Line Edition. 1 vol., 12mo, illustrated, cloth, gilt, gilt edges......................$1 25

Of all the translations of Dante, Cary's has been conceded the most successful. It is executed with perfect fidelity and admirable skill. It would be impossible to transfer the lines of the great Italian poet into our language with any closer preservation of their beauties of rhythm and meaning than Mr. Cary has succeeded in accomplishing.

Detlef (Carl).

Irene; or, the Lonely Manor. By CARL DETLEF. 1 vol., 16mo, cloth, black and gold..50 cts. Also, in paper covers, in Lovell's Library, No. 29....................20 cts.

De Quincy (Thomas).

The Spanish Nun. By THOMAS DE QUINCY. 16mo, paper covers, Lovell's Library, No. 20..10 cts.

Dickens-Collins Xmas Stories.

No Thoroughfare and Two Idle Apprentices. By CHARLES DICKENS and WILKIE COLLINS. 1 vol., 12mo, cloth, black and gold, $1 00

Dickens (Charles).

CHARLES DICKENS' COMPLETE WORKS. Lovell's Popular Illustrated Edition. Printed from entirely new electrotype plates, large clear type, with over 150 illustrations by Phiz, Barnard, Green, etc., etc.

I. **Pickwick Papers.**
II. **David Copperfield.**
III. **Martin Chuzzlewit.**
IV. **Nicholas Nickleby.**
V. **Bleak House.**
VI. **Little Dorrit.**
VII. **Dombey and Son.**
VIII. **Our Mutual Friend.**
IX. **Oliver Twist, Pictures** from **Italy,** and **American Notes.**
X. **Old Curiosity Shop** and **Hard Times.**
XI. **Tale of Two Cities** and **Sketches by Boz.**
XII. **Barnaby Rudge** and **Mystery of Edwin Drood.**

Dickens (Charles)—CONTINUED.

XIII. **Great Expectations, Uncommercial Traveller, and Miscellaneous.**
XIV. **Christmas Stories** and **Reprinted Pieces.**
XV. **Child's History of England and Miscellaneous.**

15 vols., 12mo, cloth, gilt...$22 50
15 vols., 12mo, half Russia.. 33 00
15 vols., 12mo, half calf... 45 00
Also published separately.

Child's History of England. By CHARLES DICKENS. 1 vol., 12mo, cloth, black and gold $1 00
Oliver Twist. By CHARLES DICKENS. 1 vol., 12mo, cloth, black and gold.. $1 00
Also, in paper covers, Lovell's Library No. 10.....................20 cts.
A Tale of Two Cities. By CHARLES DICKENS. 1 vol., 12mo, cloth, black and gold... $1 00
Also in paper covers, Lovell's Library No. 38.....................20 cts.

Dictionary of the Bible.
By EDWARD ROBINSON, D.D., with a history of the Bible, by WILLIAM SMITH, LL.D. 1 vol., 12mo, cloth, gilt..... ....$1 25

Don Quixote de la Mancha.
Translated from the Spanish of MIGUEL DE CERVANTES SAAVEDRA. By CHARLES JARVIS. Carefully revised and corrected. Printed from new plates, large clear type, illustrated. 1 vol., 12mo, cloth, gilt, $1 00

Doré Gallery.
The Doré Gallery of Bible Stories, illustrating the principal events in the Old and New Testaments, with descriptive Text by JOSEPHINE POLLARD. 1 large 4to volume, magnificently illustrated by Gustave Doré. Cloth, gilt..$3 00

Dryden (John).
The Poetical Works of JOHN DRYDEN. Red Line Edition.
1 vol., 12mo, illustrated, cloth, gilt, gilt edges....................$1 25

To read him is as bracing as a northwest wind. He blows the mind clear. In ripeness and bluff heartiness of expression he takes rank with the best. . To be among the first in any kind of writing, as Dryden certainly was, is to be one of a very small company.—John Russell Lowell.

Eliot (George), Works of
The Complete Works of GEORGE ELIOT, beautifully printed from large, clear type, on good paper, and handsomely bound in cloth.
8 vols., 12mo, cloth, black and gold...............................$10 00
8 vols., " on better paper, cloth, gilt top........................ 12 00
8 vols., " " half calf.................................... 24 00

I. **Middlemarch.**
II. **Daniel Deronda.**
III. **Romola.**
IV. **Felix Holt.**
V. **Romola.**
VI. **The Mill on the Floss.**
VII. **Scenes from Clerical Life and Silas Marner.**
VIII. **The Spanish Gypsy,** Jubal and other Poems, and Theophrastus Such.

Eliot (George).—CONTINUED.

Also published separately.
Adam Bede. By GEORGE ELIOT. 1 vol., 12mo, cloth, black and gold............$1 00
Also in paper covers, in two parts, Lovell's Library No. 56, each.......15 cts.

English Men of Letters.

English Men of Letters, edited by JOHN MORLEY. A series of Brief Biographies by the most eminent literary men of the day. 5 vols., 12mo. Printed from fine clear type, on good paper, handsomely bound in cloth, gilt............$3 75
Any volume sold separately, bound in cloth, gilt............75 cts.

Vol. I. contains
Burns, by Principal Shairp.
Byron, by Professor Nichol.
Milton, by Mark Pattison.
Shelley, by J. A. Symonds.

Vol. III. contains
Bunyan, by J. A. Froude.
Spenser, by the Dean of St. Paul's.
Locke, by Thomas Fowler.
Wordsworth, by F. Myers.

Vol. II. contains
Chaucer, by Prof. A. W. Ward.
Cowper, by Goldwin Smith.
Pope, by Leslie Stephen.
Southey, by Prof. Dowden.

Vol. IV. contains
Burke, by John Morley.
Gibbon, by J. C. Morison.
Hume, by Prof. Huxley.
Johnson, by Leslie Stephen.

Volume V. contains
Defoe, by William Minto.
Goldsmith, by William Black.
Scott, by R. H. Hutton.
Thackeray, by Anthony Trollope.

Each Biography is also issued separately, in neat paper cover, price, including postage, 10 cents, viz.:—

Bunyan, by J. A. Froude.
Burke, by John Morley.
Burns, by Principal Shairp.
Byron, by Professor Nichol.
Chaucer, by Prof. A. W. Ward.
Cowper, by Goldwin Smith.
Defoe, by William Minto.
Gibbon, by J. C. Morison.
Goldsmith, by William Black.
Hume, by Professor Huxley.
Johnson, by Leslie Stephen.

Locke, by Thomas Fowler.
Milton, by Mark Pattison.
Pope, by Leslie Stephen.
Scott, by R. H. Hutton.
Shelley, by J. Symonds.
Southey, by Prof. Dowden.
Spenser, by the Dean of St. Paul's.
Thackeray, by Anthony Trollope.
Wordsworth, by F. Myers.

Farrar (F. W., D.D.) Works of

Seekers after God. By F. W. FARRAR, D.D. 1 vol., 16mo, cloth, black and gold............50 cts.
Also in paper covers, Lovell's Library No. 19............20 cts.
Early Days of Christianity. By F. W. FARRAR, D.D. 1 vol., 12mo, cloth, gilt............$1 00
Also in paper covers, Lovell's Library, No. 50, in two parts, each........20 cts.

Favorite Pocket Dictionary of the English Language.

Based on the labors and principles of the latest and best American and English authorities. 1 vol., 16mo, 320 pages, cloth.........25 cts.

Favorite Poems.

Selections from the writings of the best Poets, with many poems by American authors. Red Line Edition. 1 vol., 12mo, cloth, gilt, gilt edges..$1 25

The most popular poems in the language have a place in this volume. Selected and edited with great care, they form a collection such as has never before been presented to the public, and one which is almost indispensable wherever the refined love for literature in its highest and most refined form exists.

Feuillet (Octave).

Marriage in High Life. By OCTAVE FEUILLET, translated by OLIVE LOGAN. 1 vol., 16mo, cloth, black and gold..............50 cts.
Also in paper covers, Lovell's Library No. 41.... ....20 cts.

Frankenstein;

Or, the Modern Prometheus. By MARY WOLLSTONECRAFT SHELLEY. 1 vol., 16mo, cloth, black and gold......................50 cts.
Also in paper covers, 12mo, 177 pages, Lovell's Library No. 5..........10 cts.

Sir Walter Scott has said:

"Frankstein" has passages which appal the mind and make the flesh creep."

While Thornton Hunt, speaking of Mrs. Shelley, says:

"Her command of History and her imiginative power, are shown in such a book as, "Valperga;" but the daring originality of her mind comes out most distinctly in her earliest published work, 'Frankenstein.'

George (Henry).

Progress and Poverty. By HENRY GEORGE. 16mo, paper covers, Lovell's Library No. 52.......................................20 cts.

Let us say, at the outset, that this is not a work to be brushed aside with lofty indifference or cool disdain. It is not the production of a visionary or a sciolist, of a meagerly equipped or ill-regulated mind. The writer has brought to his undertaking a comprehensive knowledge of the data and principles of science, and his skill in exposition and illustration attests a broad acquaintance with history and literature. Few books have, in recent years, proceeded from any American pen which have more plainly borne the marks of wide learning and strenuous thought, or which have brought to the expounding of a serious theme a happier faculty of elucidation.—New York Sun.

Gibbon (Charles).

The Golden Shaft. By CHAS. GIBBON. 1 vol., 16mo, cloth, black and gold.. . ...50 cts.
Also, in paper covers, in Lovell's Library, No. 57.................. ....20 cts.

Goldsmith (Oliver).

The Poetical Works of Oliver Goldsmith. Red Line Edition.
1 vol., 12mo, illustrated, cloth, gilt, gilt edges.....................$1 25

Vicar of Wakefield. By Oliver Goldsmith. Paper covers,
Lovell's Library, No. 51.................................10 cts.
Also included, in 1 vol., cloth, 12mo, with Paul and Virginia and Rasselas,$1 00

Goldsmith, both in prose and verse, is one of the most delightful writers in the language. His verse flows like a limped stream. His Traveller is one of the most finished and noble poems ever written. His Deserted Village is a masterpiece, full of an accuracy of nature, in one of its sweetest phases, and a profound pathos inexpressibly touching and powerful.

Grant (James).

The Secret Dispatch. By James Grant. 1 vol., 16mo,
cloth, black and gold...................................50 cts.
Also in paper covers, Lovell's Library No. 49....................20 cts.

Grimm Brothers.

Grimm's Popular Tales. Collected by the Brothers Grimm.
Printed from new plates, large, clear type, handsomely illustrated. 1 vol.,
12mo, cloth, black and gold..........................$1 00

Gulliver's Travels and Baron Munchausen.

Gulliver's Travels. By Dean Swift, to which is added **The Travels and Surprising Adventures of Baron Munchausen.** 2 vols. in one, 12mo. Illustrated, cloth, black and gold.................$1 00

See also Swift (Dean).

Halevy (Ludovic).

L'Abbe Constantine. By Ludovic Halevy. 1 vol., 16mo,
cloth, black and gold...................................50 cts.
Also in paper covers, Lovell's Library, No. 15...................20 cts.

Hatton (Joseph).

Clytie. A Novel. By Joseph Hatton. 1 vol., 12mo,
Lovell's Standard Library, cloth, black and gold..................$1 00
Also in Lovell's popular library, 1 vol., 16mo, cloth, extra black and gold.50 cts.
Also in paper covers, Lovell's Library, No. 7....................20 cts.

Hardy (Thomas).

Two on a Tower. By Thomas Hardy. 1 vol., 16mo, cloth,
black and gold......................................50 cts.
Also, in paper covers, Lovell's Library, No. 43..................20 cts.

Hemans (Mrs. Felicia).

The Poetical Works of Mrs. Felicia Hemans, edited with a critical Memoir by William Michael Rossetti. Illustrated by Thomas Secombe. Printed from new plates, large clear type. Red Line Edition. 1 vol., 12mo. Illustrated, cloth, gilt, gilt edges....................$1 25

Mrs. Hemans has been called the most popular of female poets. Her genius was of the domestic order, and its eminations found the safest of all abiding places, that of the family and the fireside. She shows high sentiment and heoric feeling now and then, but her affections are with the gentle, the meek and the wounded in spirit. She is the authoress of many a plaintive and mournful strain, and her poetry throughout is intensely feminine. "Her best songs," as Allan Cunningham wrote, "have been rightly named of the affections."

Henley (Leonard).
Life of Washington. By LEONARD HENLEY. 1 vol. 16mo, cloth, black and gold.. 50 cts.
Also in paper covers, Lovell's Library, No. 26............................20 cts.

Herbert (George).
The works of GEORGE HERBERT in prose and verse, edited from the latest editions, with Memoir, explanatory notes, &c. Printed from new plates, large clear type, handsomely illustrated. Red Line Edition. 1 vol., 12mo, cloth, gilt, gilt edges..$1 25

The poems of George Herbert have stood the crucial test of two centuries of criticisms and come out pure gold. With their intense devotional feeling, they combine a quaint sweetness of expression and an earnest fluency of diction which lend them a charm peculiarly their own. His homlier poems, those on which the ingenuity of his cultivated mind was not lavished, but which were thrown off as the spontaneous productions of his unconventional muse. A model of a man and a clergyman, Herbert may almost be held up as a model of a poet too.

Homer.
The Odyssey of Homer. Translated by ALEXANDER POPE, with notes and introduction by the Rev. T. A. BUCKLEY, M.A., F.S.A. Red Line Edition. With Flaxman's Designs. 1 vol., 12mo, cloth, black and gold, gilt edges...$1 25

The Iliad of Homer. Translated by ALEXANDER POPE, with notes and introduction by the Rev. T. A. BUCKLEY, M.A., F.S.A. Red Line Edition. With Flaxman's Designs. 1 vol., 12mo, cloth, black and gold, gilt edges..$1 25

Pope's translation of the Iliad was unquestionably the greatest literary labor ever executed. Dr. Johnson pronounced it the noblest version of poetry the world had ever seen, and called it a treasure of poetical elegance. It is in fact a marvelous work for purity of language and grace of style. There have been more faithful translations of Homer in the literal sense, but none which approached that of Pope in literary value.

Hood (Thomas).
The choice works of THOMAS HOOD, in Prose and Verse, including the cream of the Comic Annuals, with Life of the Author. Portrait and over 200 illustrations. 1 vol., 12mo, 780 pp., cloth............$2 00
Cheaper edition, 1 vol., 12mo, cloth, black and gold.................... 1 00
The Poetical Works of THOMAS HOOD. Red Line Edition. 1 vol., 12mo, illustrated, cloth, gilt, gilt edges....................................$1 25

Hood's verse, whether serious or comic, is ever pregnant with materials for thoughts. Like every author distinguished for true comic humor, there is a deep vein of melancholy pathos running through his mirth. The same genius that created the Lost Boy gave birth to the Song of the Shirt, the Bridge of Sighs, and the Dream of Eugene Aram. While his lighter works bristle with wit and fine sarcasm, his serious ones are pregnant with such tenderness and such sense of nature, animate and inanimate, as few poets have ever peered.

Houdin (Robert).

The Tricks of the Greeks Unveiled; or, The Art of Winning at every Game. By ROBERT HOUDIN. Translated by M. I. Smithson. 1 vol., 16mo, cloth, black and gold............................50 cts.
Also in paper covers, Lovell's Library No. 14.........................20 cts.

Ingelow (Jean).

The complete Poetical Works of JEAN INGELOW. Printed in clear type, on good paper. Red Line Edition. 1 vol., 12mo. Illustrated, cloth, gilt, gilt edges... 1 25

The world has seen few sweeter singers than Jean Ingelow. Her poetical works have obtained a circulation and a popularity equally deserved. Her love of nature has found vent in simple lays which have stolen their ways to numberless hearts, while her poetic instinct has evinced itself in works of a high order of picturesqueness and art.

Ivanhoe.

By SIR WALTER SCOTT, Bart. From the last Edinburgh edition, with the author's final notes and corrections. 1 vol. 12mo. Illustrated cloth, gilt.. 1 00

Ivanhoe was given to the world in 1820, and within the year had been translated into most European languages. "Scott's bosom," says Prescott, "warmed with a sympathetic glow for the age of chivalry. No one can form an idea of the people who moved in it, of Richard Cœur de Lion and his brave paladins, that has not read Ivanhoe."

James (G. P. R.)

One-Volume Edition. Containing a selection of the best novels of this popular writer:—

One in a Thousand.	Philip Augustus.
Richelieu.	The Gypsy.
The Robbers.	The Ancient Régime.

The Gentleman of the Old School.
1 vol., 8vo, cloth, black and gold...$2 50

Jay (Harriett).

The Dark Colleen. By HARRIETT JAY. 1 vol., 16mo, cloth, extra black and gold...50 cts.
Also in paper covers, Lovell's Library No. 17.........................20 cts.

Junius's Letters.

The Letters of Junius. WOODFALL'S edition. From the latest London edition. 1 vol. 12mo, cloth, black and gold..............$1 25

These letters of that mysterious genius Junius, whose identity is not known to this day, are reprinted from the edition issued by his own publisher, Woodfall. The classic purity of their language, the force and perspicuity of their arguments, the keen severity of their reproach, and the extensive information they evince, place these celebrated epistles in the first rank of English literature.

Keats (John).

The Poetical Works of John Keats. Red Line Edition. 1 vol., 12mo. Illustrated, cloth, gilt edges....................... ... $1 25

In his Endymion Keats created a work which the critics have not done disputing over yet, but which the reading public acknowledges to be one of the most startling, novel, and fantastically beautiful epics which the muse of any modern mortal ever formed a conception of. Two works in which Keats is seen to his best advantage are his Lamia and Isabella. These, as well as his minor poems, are all included in the above edition.

Kingsley (Charles).

The Hermits. By CHAS. KINGSLEY. 1 vol. 16mo, cloth, black and gold..50 cts.
Also in paper covers, Lovell's Library No. 39........................20 cts.
Hypatia. By CHAS. KINGSLEY. 1 vol., 16mo, cloth, black and gold............... ....50 cts.
Also in paper covers, Lovell's Library, in two parts, each........ .....15 cts

Knight (Charles).

Popular History of England, from the landing of Julius Cæsar to the death of Prince Albert. By CHARLES KNIGHT. Library Edition. 8 vols., 12mo. 160 illustrations, cloth, gilt top....... $12 00
The same, popular edition, 4 vols., 12mo. 32 illustrations, cloth, gilt... $6 00

Knight's History of England has taken its place among the standard chronicles of the world. The critics pronounced the author, in consideration of his valuable work "one of the first literary benefactors of the age." The style is easy and graceful, and free from all the ponderousness and dryness of description which render so many histories unreadable.

Lamb (Charles).

The Complete Works, in Prose and Verse, of CHARLES LAMB, from the original edition, with the cancelled passages restored, and many pieces now first collected. Edited and prefaced by A. H. SHEPHERD. 1 vol., 12mo. Illustrated, 790 pp., cloth, extra gilt.... ....$2 00

Language and Poetry of Flowers.

Language and Poetry of Flowers. Selected from the best authors. Red Line Edition. 1 vol., 12mo. Illustrated, cloth, gilt, gilt edges... ....$1 25

Last Days of Pompeii.

See LORD LYTTON.

Last of the Mohicans.

See COOPER (J. FENIMORE).

Lee (Margaret).

Divorce. By MARGARET LEE. 1 vol., 16mo, cloth, black and gold........................ ....50 cts.
Also in paper Covers, Lovell's Library, No. 25..... ....20 cts.

Life and Letters of Lord Macaulay.

By his nephew GEORGE OTTO TREVELYAN, M.P. Two volumes in one. 1 vol., 12mo., cloth, gilt $1 25

> *The personality of Macaulay is marked in his written life as clearly as he ever marked that of any of his historic heroes. The letters and papers, the fragments of the great chronicler's work thus rescued from oblivion, are a mine of interest. The reader to whom Macaulay the litterateur has become familiar through his own productions, will never know Macaulay the man until he learns him through the medium of his nephew's pen picture.*

Longfellow (H. W.) Works

Hyperion. A Romance. By H. W. Longfellow. 1 vol., 16mo, cloth, gilt.... ....50 cts.
Also in paper covers, Lovell's Library, No. 1................ ....20 cts.

Outre-Mer. A Pilgrimage beyond the Sea. By H. W. LONGFELLOW. 1 vol., 16mo, cloth, gilt......................................50 cts.
Also in paper covers, Lovell's Library, No. 2........................20 cts.

Lovell's Red Line Poets.

Lovell's Red Line Edition of the Poets. Without doubt the finest and most complete edition of the poets ever issued in this country, at a low price. In 12mo volumes, illustrated, handsomely bound in cloth, black and gold, gilt edges..$1 25

Arnold.	Goldsmith.	Pope.
Aytoun.	Hemans.	Procter.
Burns.	Hood.	Religious Poems.
Byron.	Herbert.	Schiller.
Browning.	Iliad.	Scott.
Chaucer.	Ingelow.	Shakspeare.
Campbell.	Keats.	Shelley.
Cowper.	Kirke White.	Spenser.
Crabbe.	Lucile.	Taylor's Philip van
Coleridge.	Milton.	Artevald.
Dante.	Moore.	Tennyson.
Dryden.	Macaulay.	Thomson.
Eliot.	Meredith.	Tupper.
Eliza Cook.	Ossian.	Virgil.
Favorite Poems.	Odyssey	White, Kirke.
Goethe.	Poe.	Willis.
Goethe's Faust.	Poetry of Flowers.	Wordsworth.

Lovell's Library,

Under the title of "LOVELL'S LIBRARY; A WEEKLY PUBLICATION," the undersigned have commenced the publication of all the best works in Current and Standard Literature. It is believed that this issue will be found superior to anything heretofore attempted, especially in the following points: *First*—The type will be larger and the print consquently clearer. *Second*—The size being the popular 12mo, will be found much more pleasant and convenient to handle. *Third*—Each number will have a handsome paper cover; and this, in connection with the size, will make it worthy of preservation.

NUMBERS NOW READY:

CENTS.
1. **Hyperion**, by Longfellow, 20
2. **Outre-Mer**, by Longfellow.................. 20
3. **The Happy Boy**, by Björnson............. 10
4. **Arne**, by Björnson...... 10
5. **Frankenstein**, by Mrs. Shelley.............. 10
6. **The Last of the Mohicans**................. 20
7. **Clytie**, by Joseph Hatton, 20
8. **The Moonstone**, by Wilkie Collins, Part I..... 10
9. Do. Part II............ 10
10. **Oliver Twist**, by Dickens, 20
11. **The Coming Race;** or the New Utopia, by Lord Lytton.............. 10
12. **Leila;** or the Siege of Granada, by Lord Lytton, 10
13. **The Three Spaniards**, by George Walker..... 20
14. **The Tricks of the Greeks Unveiled**, by Robert Houdin................... 20
15. **L'Abbe Constantin**, by Ludovic Halévy, author of "La Fille de Mme. Angot," etc........... 20
16. **Freckles**, by Rebecca Fergus Redcliff. A new original story.............. 20

CENTS.
17. **The Dark Colleen**, by Mrs. Robert Buchanan, 20
18. **They were Married**, by Walter Besant and James Rice................. 10
19. **Seekers after God**, by Canon Farrar.......... 20
20. **The Spanish Nun**, by Thos. De Quincey...... 10
21. **The Green Mountain Boys**, by Judge D. P. Thompson............ 20
22. **Fleurette**, by Eugene Scribe................ 20
23. **Second Thoughts**, by Rhoda Broughton 20
24. **The New Magdalen**, by Wilkie Collins......... 20
25. **Divorce**, by Margaret Lee, 20
26. **Life of Washington**, by Leonard Henley....... 20
27. **Social Etiquette**, by Mrs. W. A. Saville ... 15
28. **Single Heart and Double Face**, by Chas. Reade.. 10
29. **Irene;** or, the Lonely Manor................ 20
30. **Vice-Versa**, by F. Anstey, 20
31. **Ernest Maltravers**, by Lord Lytton.......... 20

Lovell's Library—CONTINUED.

	CENTS.
32. **The Haunted House** and Calderon the Courtier, by Lord Lytton	10
33. **John Halifax**, by Miss Mulock	20
34. **800 Leagues on the Amazon**, by Jules Verne	10
35. **The Cryptogram**, by Jules Verne	10
36. **Life of Marion**, by Horry and Weems	20
37. **Paul and Virginia**	10
38. **Tale of Two Cities**, by Charles Dickens	20
39. **The Hermits**, by Rev. Charles Kingsley	20
40. **An Adventure in Thule**, and Marriage of Moira Fergus, by Wm. Black	10
41. **A Marriage in High Life**, by Octave Feuillet	20
42. **Robin**, by Mrs. Parr	20
43. **Two on a Tower**, by Thomas Hardy	20
44. **Rasselas**, by Samuel Johnson	10
45. **Alice; or the Mysteries**, being Part II. of Ernest Maltravers	20
46. **Duke of Kandos**, by A. Mathey	20
47. **Baron Munchausen**	10
48. **A Princess of Thule**, by Wm. Black	20
49. **The Secret Despatch**, Grant	20
50. **Early Days of Christianity**, by Canon Farrar, D.D., Part I	20
Do. Part II	20
51. **Vicar of Wakefield**, by Oliver Goldsmith	10

	CENTS.
52. **Progress and Poverty**, by Henry George	20
53. **The Spy**, by J. Fenimore Cooper	20
54. **East Lynne**, by Mrs. Henry Wood	20
55. **A Strange Story**, by Lord Lytton	20
56. **Adam Bede**, by George Eliot, Part I	15
Do. Part II	15
57. **The Golden Shaft**, by Charles Gibbon	20
58. **Portia: or by Passions Rocked**, by "The Duchess"	20
59. **Last Days of Pompeii**, by Lord Lytton	20
60. **The Two Duchesses**, by A. Mathey	20
Hypatia, by Rev. Charles Kingsley, Part I	15
Do. Part II	15
The Vendetta. Tales of Love and Passion, by Honoré de Balzac	20
Gulliver's Travels, by Dean Swift	20
Horse Shoe Robinson, by Kennedy, Part I	15
Do. Part II	15
Jane Eyre, by Charlotte Brontë	20
The Wooing O't, by Mrs. Alexander, Part I	15
Do. Part II	15
The Admiral's Ward, by Mrs. Alexander	20
John Wynne's Wives, by C. M. Clay, author of "The Modern Hagar,"	20

Lovell's Popular Library.

In 16mo volumes, handsomely bound in cloth, black and gold, 50 cents each.

BY F. ANSTEY.
Vice-Versa.

BY MRS. ALEXANDER.
The Admiral's Ward.
In Press.
The Wooing, O. T.

BY BJORNST. BJORNSON.
The Happy Boy, and Arne.

BY WILLIAM BLACK.
A Princess of Thule.

BY CHARLOTTE BRONTE.
Jane Eyre.

AY RHODA BROUGHTON.
Second Thoughts.

BY WILKIE COLLINS.
The Moonstone.
The New Magdalen.

PY CARL DETLEF.
Irene: or the Lonely Manor.

By REV. CANON FARRAR, D.D.
Seekers after God.

BY OCTAVE FEUILLET.
Marriage in High Life.

BY CHARLES GIBBON.
The Golden Shaft.

BY JAMES GRANT.
The Secret Dispatch.

BY LUDOVIC HALEVY.
L'Abbe Constantine.

BY THOMAS HARDY.
Two on a Tower.

BY JOSEPH HATTON.
Clytie.

BY LEONARD HENLEY.
Life of Washington.

BY HORRY AND WEEMS.
Life of Marion.

ROBERT HOUDIN.
The Tricks of the Greeks Unveiled.

BY HARRIETT JAY.
The Dark Colleen.

BY REV. CHARLES KINGSLEY.
Hypatia.
The Hermits.

BY MARGARET LEE.
Divorce.

BY H. W. LONGFELLOW.
Hyperion.
Outre-Mer.

BY LORD LYTTON.
The Coming Race: or the New Utopia, and Leila: or the Siege of Granada.

BY A. MATHEY.
Duke of Kandos.
The Two Duchesses.

BY MISS MULOCK.
John Halifax.

BY MRS. PARR.
Robin.

BY REBECCA FERGUS REDDCLIFF.
Freckles.

BY EUGENE SCRIBE.
Fleurette.

BY MARY WOLSTONECRAFT SHELLEY.
Frankenstien; or the Modern Prometheus, to which is added The Haunted House and Calderon the Courtier, by LORD LYTTON.

BY JUDGE D. P. THOMPSON.
The Green Mountain Boys.

BY JULES VERNE.
The Giant Raft. Part I., 800 Leagues on the Amazon; Part II. The Cryptogram.

BY GEORGE WALKER.
The Three Spaniards.

BY MRS. HENRY WOOD.
East Lynne.

Lovell's Standard Library.

The best selection of Classic Fiction, etc. Printed uniformly in large clear type, from new electrotype plates, and very beautifully bound. Sold at the uniform price of $1 a volume, making this edition the most desirable in the market. In 12mo volumes. Cloth, black and gold per volume $1 00

First Series.

Robinson Crusoe.
Arabian Nights.
Swiss Family Robinson.
Children of the Abbey.
Don Quixote.
Bunyan's Pilgrim's Progress.
Ivanhoe.
Scottish Chiefs.
Thaddeus of Warsaw.
Last Days of Pompeii.
Andersen's Fairy Tales.

Tom Brown's School Days at Rugby.
Grimm's Popular Tales.
Paul and Virginia, Rasselas, and the Vicar of Wakefield.
Gulliver's Travels and Baron Munchausen.
Dicken's Childs History of England.
Willy Reilly.

Second Series.

Vanity Fair.
The Mysterious Island—JULES VERNE.
20,000 Leagus under the Sea.
Tour of the World in 80 days.
The Fur Country. — JULES VERNE.
Five Weeks in a Baloon.— JULES VERNE.
Last of the Mohicans.

Irving's Sketch Book.
Oliver Twist.
Dickens-Collins Xmas Stories.
Waverley.
Redgauntlet.
Clytie.
John Halifax.
East Lynne.
Jane Eyre.
Adam Bede.

Lucile.

By OWEN MEREDITH. Printed from new plates, large clear type. Red Line Edition. 1 vol., 12mo. Illustrated, cloth, gilt, gilt edges....... ....$1 25

Lytton (Lord).

Last Days of Pompeii. By SIR EDWARD BULWER, LORD
Lytton, Lovell's Standard Classics. 1 vol., 12mo. Illustrated, cloth, black
and gold..$1 00
Also in paper covers, Lovell's Library, No. 59.........................20 cts.

*The Last Days of Pompeii is a picture of the life of that extinct city which
even the researches of modern archæology have not created the equal of. The
extraordinary faculty Bulwer possessed of reviving from the dry pages of
history the real spirit of the times it deals with, is fully established in this
story. No words ever painted a grander and more inspiring picture than the
eruption of Vesuvius, under which the gay city perished in the bloom of its existence, with which the story finds its end.*

The Coming Race; or, **The New Utopia, and Leila,** or **the
Siege of Granada.** By LORD LYTTON. 1 vol., 16mo, cloth, black and
gold...50 cts.
Also published separately as Nos. 11 and 12 Lovell's Library, paper covers,
each...10 cts.

Ernest Maltravers. By LORD LYTTON. Paper covers,
Lovell's Library, No. 31...20 cts.

Alice; or, The Mysteries. Sequel to Ernest Maltravers. By
LORD LYTTON. Paper covers, No. 45, Lovell's Library............20 cts.

The Haunted House and Calderon the Courtier. By
LORD LYTTON. Paper covers, Lovell's Library, No. 32.............10 cts

A Strange Story. By LORD LYTTON. 16mo, plain paper
covers, Lovell's Library, No. 55......................................20 cts.

Macaulay (Thomas Babington).

History of England, from the Accession of James the Second.
By THOMAS BABINGTON MACAULAY. This is a new edition of this well-
known Standard Work, printed from new electrotype plates, in the popular
12mo form, and is without doubt the best of the cheaper editions of the work
published. 5 vols., 12mo, 600 pp. each, cloth, in box................$5 00

*Macaulay's History of England has been justly called a great national
work. Its power, wisdom and success command unfeigned admiration. Every
page bears testimony to a degree of conscientious and minute research which no
historian has ever surpassed, and few have ever approached. The work is a
monument to a life of indefatigable toil. The style is faultlessly luminous;
every word is in its right place; every sentence is exquisitely balanced; the
current of interest never flags. More than 150,000 were sold in this country in
the first month after publication.*

Critical and Miscellaneous Essays and Poems. Fine large
type, new stereotype plates, printed on good paper, neatly bound, 3 vols.,
12mo. 820 pp. each...$3 75

*" They rank among the finest artistic products of the century.........The
amount of knowledge each of them includes can only be estimated by those who
have patiently read the many volumes they so brilliantly condense."—Edwin
P. Whipple.*

Complete Works, consisting of the above five volumes of the
History, and three volumes of the Critical and Miscellaneous Essays and
Poems. 8 vols., 12mo, cloth, in box..................................$8 00

Macaulay (Thomas) Babington—CONTINUED.

Lays of Ancient Rome, with Ivry, the Armada, and other Poems, By LORD MACAULAY. Red Line Edition. 1 vol., 12mo. Illustrated cloth, gilt, gilt edges........ ....$1 25

The "Lays of Ancient Rome," the vividness of outline, graphic breadth and rapidity of narrative, approach the poems of Scott. The "Battle of the Bridge" is full of heroic action and energy, and "Virginia" is touching from the very simplicity of its majestic sentiment. Macaulay as a poet rivals Macaulay as a historian. If he had written much more verse he still would not have penned enough.

Life and Letters of Lord Macaulay, by his nephew GEORGE OTTO TREVELYAN, M.P. Two volumes in one. 1 vol., 12mo. 630 pages, cloth, gilt...... ....$1 25

Mathey (A.)

Duke of Kandos. By A. MATHEY, translated by FRANK P. CLARK. 1 vol., 16mo, cloth, extra, black and gold..................50 cts.
Also in paper covers, Lovell's Library, No. 46......................20 cts.

The Two Duchesses. By A. MATHEY, translated by FRANK P. CLARK, 1 vol., 16mo, cloth, black and gold......... .... 50 cts.
Also in paper covers, Lovell's Library, No. 58......... ....20 cts.

Meredith, Owen (Robert Lord Lytton).

The Poetical Works of OWEN MEREDITH (ROBERT LORD LYTTON). Printed from new electrotype plates, handsomely illustrated. Red Line Edition. 1 vol., 12mo. Illustrated, cloth, gilt, gilt edges. $1 25

Since the publication of his first work, Clytemnestry Meredith has steadily ascended in the scale of poetic rank. He has the spirit and feeling of the genuine poet improved by the judgment of the man of the world, and the condition of the scholar. No brighter or more charming verses have ever been written than some of those which make up Owen Meredith's volume.

Lucile. By OWEN MEREDITH. Printed from new plates, large clear type. Red Line Edition. 1 vol., 12mo. Illustrated, cloth, gilt, gilt edges.............................. ....$1 25

Milton (John).

The Poetical Works of JOHN MILTON, with a Life. Red Line Edition. 1 vol., 12mo. Illustrated, cloth, gilt, gilt edges $1 25

Moore (Thomas).

The Poetical Works of THOMAS MOORE, with Memoir and full explanatory notes. Printed from new electrotype plates, handsomely illustrated. Red Line Edition. 1 vol., 12mo. Illustrated, cloth, gilt, gilt edges $1 25

Every person with one note of music in his soul should own a copy of this book Though in one respect Moore is a universal poet, in that his works are household treasures in almost every home; yet is he par excellence, the Poet of the Emerald Isle.

JUST PUBLISHED:

SCIENCE IN SHORT CHAPTERS

By W. MATTIEU WILLIAMS, F.R.A.S. F.C.S.

Author of " The Fuel of the Sun," " A Simple Treatise on Heat," &c.

BEING No. 80 OF LOVELL'S LIBRARY,

12mo, handsome paper covers, **Price, 20 Cents.**

"Mr. Mattieu Williams is undoubtedly able to present scientific subjects to the popular mind with much clearness and force; and these essays may be read with advantage by those, who, without having had special training, are yet sufficiently intelligent to take interest in the movement of events in the scientific world."—*Academy.*

"The title of Mr. Mattieu Williams' 'Science in Short Chapters' exactly explains its subject. Clear and simple, these brief reprints from all sorts of periodicals are just what Angelina may profitably read to Edwin while he is sorting his papers, or trimming the lamps, if (like some highly domesticated Edwins) he insists on doing that tickl sh bit of house-work himself."—*Graphic.*

"The papers are not mere rechauffés of common knowledge. Almost all of them are marked by original thought, and many of them contain demonstrations or aperçus of considerable scientific value."—*Pall Mall Gazette.*

"The chapte s range from such subjects as science and spiritualism to the consumption of sm ke. They include a dissertation on iron filings in tea, and they discuss the action of frost on water-pipes and on building materials. The volume begins with an article on the fuel of the sun, and before it is concluded it deals with Count Rumford's cooking stoves. All these subjects, and a great many more, are treated in a pleasant, informative manner. Mr. Williams knows what he is talking about, and he says what he ha to say in such a way as to prevent any possible misconception. The book will be prized by all who desire to have sound information on such subjects as those with which it deals."—*Scotsman.*

"To the scientific world Mr. Williams is best known by his solar studies, but here he is not writing so much for scientists as for the general public. It has been the aim of his life to popularise science, and his articles are so treated that his readers may become interested in them and find in their perusal a mental recreation."—*Sunday-school Chronicle.*

"We highly recommend this most entertaining and vauable collection of papers. They combine clearness and simplicity, and are not wanting in philosophy likewise."—*Tablet.*

LIFE OF OLIVER CROMWELL,

His Life, Times, Battlefields, and Contemporaries, by

PAXTON HOOD,

Author of " Christmas Evans," " Thomas Carlyle," " Romance of Biography," &c.

Being No. 73 of LOVELL'S LIBRARY,

12mo, handsome paper covers, **15 CENTS.**

This is a popular biography of the career of Oliver Cromwell, which will be welcomed by those who are unable to pursue the stirring history of his life and times, in the elaborate volumes to which the student is at present referred.

For sale by all booksellers and newsdealers, or sent free of postage on receipt of price by the publishers.

JOHN W. LOVELL CO.,
14 and 16 Vesey St., New York.

Malthoptonique

THE ENGLISH EXTRACT OF MALT AND HOPS.

Nature's Great Restorative
In all Cases of Nervous Debility

Builds up anew the enfeebled physique, overcomes the effects of **Exhaus**tion and **Nervous Excitement**, and enables those who use it to perform an increased amount of physical and mental labor. It improves the appetite, conquers **Dyspepsia**, and promotes a rapid assimilation of the food.

Wakefulness, Tremors, Twitching, Unnatural Anxiety, and other **Nervous Symptons** are obviated by its use.

"A REFRESHING NIGHT'S SLEEP IN EVERY BOTTLE."—(*Commerce Advertiser.*)

Read what prominent physicians in different sections of the country say regarding this Delightful and Refreshing Tonic Drink:

"We have used Burton's Malthoptonique in our practice in cases Nervous Disorders, and have found it among the best remedial agents have ever tried for that class of diseases.

"J. A. BROWN, M. D.   D O. FARRAND, M. D.   GEO. A. FOSTER, M.
J. F. NOYES, M. D.   D. NORTON, M. D."

Five prominent Physicians in Detroit, Mich.

NEWARK, N. J., Oct. 19th, 1882.

"During the past two years I have frequently prescribed 'BURTON's MALTHOPTONIQU and used it in my family with very satisfactory results.

"It is particularly efficacious in relieving sleeplessness, and I find it a pleasant and liable tonic in all cases of debility."

LESLIE D. WARD, M. D.

"I consider BURTON's MALTHOPTONIQUE a very valuable Remedy for building patients who have become eufeeb ed by disease or suffering Nervous Prostration."

NEWARK, N. J.   GEO. S. WARD, M. D.

"I have tried BURTON'S MALTHOPTONIQUE personally, and have had occasion frequen to prescribe it in my practice, and may recommend it because of its tonic and soothi qualities, especially in nervous insomnia."

DR. G. FRAUENSTEIN, 359 W. 15th St., New York.

Sold by Druggists and Grocers generally, throughout the United States.

E. C. HAZARD & CO., Sole Agents,

192 *Chambers St., New York*

www.ingramcontent.com/pod-product-compliance
Lightning Source LLC
Chambersburg PA
CBHW032103230426
43672CB00009B/1618